# 150 YEARS LATER
## *Broken Ties Mended*

## MELVIN J. COLLIER

ISBN-10: 146372568X
ISBN-13: 978-1463725686

*Write Here Publishing*
*www.WriteHerePublishing.com*
This book can be ordered at www.150yearslater.com.

Cover design by Melvin J. Collier and Roylee Cummings

Printed in the United States of America

# Dedication

In loving memory of

## Isaac "Ike" Deberry Sr.
### *October 12, 1914 – October 8, 2009*

Without his remarkable memory, his great love for family, his passionate love for family history, and his cherished relationship with his maternal grandfather William "Bill" Reed, *150 Years Later, Broken Ties Mended* would not have been possible. Rest in peace, Cousin Ike.

# Contents

*Introduction* • i

Chapter 1 – "The feeling was just there." • 1

Chapter 2 – "What a great griot he was!" • 25

Chapter 3 – Gone but not forgotten. • 39

Chapter 4 – Reid not Reed • 63

Chapter 5 – "They were his people." • 87

Chapter 6 – The Mysterious Mother • 99

Chapter 7 – What happened to them? • 107

Chapter 8 – More Revelations • 119

Chapter 9 – "The negroes are to be divided." • 135

Chapter 10 – The Ties That Bind • 143

Chapter 11 – "Back to Caroliny" • 167

Chapter 12 – "Let No Man Put Asunder." • 185

*Epilogue* • 213

*Acknowledgments* • 215

*Endnotes* • 217

*Index* • 227

# Introduction

*O n one of these sale days, I saw a mother lead seven children to the auction block. She knew that some of them would be taken from her; but they took all. The children were sold to a slave-trader, and their mother was bought by a man in her own town. Before night her children were all far away. She begged the trader to tell her where he intended to take them; this he refused to do. How could he, when he knew he would sell them, one by one, wherever he could command the highest price? She wrung her hands in anguish, and exclaimed, "Gone! All gone! Why doesn't God kill me?"* – Harriet Jacobs[1]

After the Civil War's end, many emancipated African Americans sought tirelessly for their family members from whom they were torn asunder. They often thought of them, like William "Bill" Reed had done with a heavy heart, wondering about his family's whereabouts. In South Carolina, when my great-grandfather was twelve years old, he watched his father being sold away, never to see him again, and he helplessly watched as his mother, grandmother, brother, and other family members were taken away, never to lay eyes on them again as well. Bill and a younger sister named Mary were then sold to a local owner. However, he never forgot his family. His soul would not allow him to forget them.

Family remained crucially important to Bill, as revealed by his decision to name his youngest son after his long-lost father. Family was paramount, as evident by the many stories he shared with his children and grandchildren underneath his sycamore tree on his 300-plus-acre farm near Senatobia, Mississippi. As a storyteller, Bill continued to share his childhood memories of his slavery days in South Carolina until his demise in 1937, at the age of ninety-one. He wanted his family to know from whence he had come.

*150 Years Later* tells Bill Reed's stories. His stories and my family's willingness to share them ultimately led to his mysterious history being unraveled and also redeemed in a grand fashion – an emotional and powerful family reunion that occurred 150 years after his family unit was dismantled. His stories displayed the terrible burdens chattel slavery had placed on the stability of African-American families. His stories also revealed the centrality of family in his life, as well as the lives of other former slaves who were always under the dreadful threat of being forever separated from their kin. From his stories, *150 Years Later* also demonstrates the great value in oral history and the importance of capturing it.

In order to fully understand why Bill Reed and many other former slaves placed such a high value on family and to appreciate its importance, one must revert back to the roots – Africa. Inside a small region of a massively beautiful continent, stretching from Senegal to Angola, the ancestors of African Americans hailed from culturally rich communities where the family was the foundation for the survival and growth of the village. Traditional African societies were diverse in many ways, but a cultural feature shared by nearly all of them was that life was centered around the family – often an extensive kinship network that included all who descended from a common male or female ancestor. It did not matter if an ancestor was from the Akan culture of Ghana, the Yoruba culture of Nigeria, or the Mende culture of Sierra Leone, their familial ideologies were similar regarding family life, and those cultural values accompanied them to North and South America.

In spite of the physical and psychological trauma those chained ancestors would come to endure on this side of the Atlantic Ocean, the institution of family never waned. Its importance among African Americans continued on after slavery, during Reconstruction, throughout the Jim Crow era, the Great Migration, the Civil Rights Movement era, and up to the present. In the midst of the many injustices African Americans faced in society, the family was crucial in providing moral, psychological, and financial support, not only to consanguineal family members, but also to many unrelated individuals who were considered a member of the family. Family support enabled many former slaves to endure the atrocities of chattel slavery – if they were fortunate to be among their family members on farms and plantations throughout the South.

Bill Reed's stories are an attest that people of African descent are not ethnically wired to be individualists. The tradition of family must and should continue in churches, schools, communities, and most importantly, in immediate and extended families. Aspects of modern society and thinking should not be allowed to erode the cultural essence of family that was undoubtedly brought over from Africa. *150 Years Later* displays that powerful essence – one that should never die.

**William "Bill" Reed**
*(September 1846 – November 31, 1937)*
Sketch created by George Geder

# Chapter 1

## "The feeling was just there."

*I* was only four years old when *Roots* aired on national television in January 1977. Surprisingly, I recalled my family being glued to the television as if they were watching something they had never seen. In reality, it was. Despite my youth, I still ascertained that *Roots* was something phenomenal, something that would have long-lasting effects, not only for my family but for many African-American families. The twelve-hour television miniseries, based on Alex Haley's best-selling novel *Roots*, followed seven generations in the lives of an enslaved family. The saga began with Kunta Kinte, a West African youth from the Gambia who was captured by slave raiders and shipped to Annapolis, Maryland in 1767. My parents were among the nearly 130 million Americans who were galvanized by the story, one that has since been deemed a work of fiction. Regardless of its validity, *Roots* opened the eyes of many to the inhumanities of chattel slavery in America, and it piqued the interest of many African Americans concerning their own family history.

Ten years later, while sitting at the kitchen table, Mom observed that I had something on my mind. I was in deep thought. For Black History Month, my ninth grade history teacher, Mrs. Bertha Howard, had shown an episode of *Roots* to the class earlier that day, so I was thinking about my own roots that night. All of Mom's grandparents died before she was born, but fortunately she knew their names.

With curiosity, I peppered her with questions. "What was your grandfather's name, your Dad's father," I asked.

Relieved that I didn't have any bad news, Mom shared, "His name was Bill Reed. He died before I was born, but my father and Aunt John would tell us about him." Aunt John Ella Reed Bobo was one of my grandfather's younger sisters.

I continued, "Was he a slave?"

"Yes, he and Momma Sarah were both born during those times. I believe Daddy said that he was originally from the Carolinas."

Fascinated by this oral history, I questioned further, "North Carolina or South Carolina?"

"I believe it was South Carolina. I'll have to ask Eartha to be sure. Aunt John talked about him quite often, and she would tell us that he had been a slave," Mom shared. Aunt Eartha, my mother's sister, verified that their grandfather had come from South Carolina.

I was a young teenager in 1987, and I was the great-grandson of former slaves. Moreover, I had not fathomed that I had roots outside of Mississippi, other than the distant Motherland. Those facts captivated me. Some of my friends, classmates, and many teenagers my age had great-grandparents still living. However, Mom's paternal grandparents were long gone; if they had been living when I was born, they would have been well over a hundred years old.

Mom's father, Simpson A. Reed, came into the world on Valentine's Day in 1881 in Tate County, Mississippi. No one knows for sure what the "A" in his middle name stood for, but he signed "S. A. Reed" on his last marriage license, dated February 17, 1936. At the age of fifty-five, he married my much-younger grandmother, Minnie Lee

Davis, who was twenty-seven years younger. Her father, John Hector Davis, who died months before her marriage, had approved of her courtship with Granddaddy Simpson, who was just ten years younger than "Poppa John." Their family blossomed to six children, four boys and two girls. My grandparents' youngest daughter was my nurturing mother. Granddaddy Simpson was the reason why I was only three generations from slavery. He was an active, hardworking elderly man during his children's teenage years. He was also a loving father and his children adored him. In their eyes, he was a saint.

According to his children, Granddaddy Simpson was not a big talker, a trait that was passed on to my mother and ultimately to me. However, when he spoke, people listened, especially members of Beulah Baptist Church near Como, Mississippi, where he was an esteemed deacon. Mom shared, "When it came to making decisions regarding certain issues involving the congregation, the members seem to have thought that his words were both 'law and gospel.' His mannerism was that of calmness, patience, gentleness, and his soft spoken words often captured the attention of people who didn't really know him."

She further reminisced, "I remember on many Sunday afternoons, my father's church friends, especially the deacons, would come by and share a Sunday dinner. After dinner, they would do Bible study. Usually, my mother would do the reading and the group would discuss the scriptures. When questions regarding interpretation of certain scriptures were needed, they would depend on him to give the interpretation. He was always alert and had a great understanding of the scriptures."

My uncles often share with pride the day their father stood up to a white man in the 1950s – something that was rarely and cautiously done in Mississippi, especially during that time. Many African Americans had been killed, lynched, or ran out of the state for this and for many false allegations. Between the end of Reconstruction to the beginning of the Great Depression, 2,018 separate incidents of lynching occurred in which at least 2,462 African-American men, women, and children met their deaths at the hand of southern mobs. Of the ten southern states, Mississippi had the highest number of lynchings; the lynching rate surpassed its neighbors, Alabama, Louisiana, Tennessee and Arkansas, by more than forty percent.[1]

Uncle Leon, Uncle Sonny, and Uncle Melvin were young boys who were helping their father clear some of his acreage. Granddaddy Simpson owned and farmed nearly two hundred acres of land. My young uncles were given the audacious task of burning some of the trees and bushes that had been cut. To their misfortune, the fire got a little out of hand and spread onto their neighbor Paul White's property.

Paul White was not a happy camper. He came out in anger and shouted to my uncles, "Look at this damn fire! I ought to give you boys a good whipping for this!"

They recalled their father's courageous response, "Oh, no you won't! I do not mind paying you for any damage that was done, but you ain't gonna lay one finger on them. These are my boys, and I speak for them!" That episode continues to be my uncles' favorite memory of their father's unbreakable strength.

Granddaddy Simpson wanted to become a medical doctor, according to his children, but that opportunity was infrequent during the 1910s, when he was a young man in Mississippi. However, he loved and stressed education and ultimately married schoolteachers. My grandmother Minnie was his second wife. Like so many other African-American men during that time frame, he made a living in agriculture. He benefitted greatly by having his own land rather than sharecropping, which was essentially neo-slavery in many forms. Granddaddy Simpson had inherited some of his land from his father and purchased adjacent tracts from the Moores. Apparently, he prospered as a farmer because he often loaned money to family members and friends. Although he was a quiet-natured man, people knew not to double-cross him and promptly paid him back if they wanted his trust in loaning money to them again.

Mom expressed, "Daddy was a very gentle man, but don't push him to the curb. If you did, he would calmly let you know how he felt about whatever the situation was, especially if he felt that you had dealt unfairly with him."

Mom talked about her father with so much love and pride that I would often ask her, "Who look like him the most?" There are no pictures of Granddaddy Simpson. The only one he was known to have taken was of him sitting on his horse. That once-treasured picture has not been located, so I have always felt this void of being oblivious to how my maternal grandfather looked. Mom and her brother, Uncle Sonny, bear a striking resemblance to my grandmother, so I glance at Aunt Eartha and their baby brother, Uncle Ed, and speculate that my grandfather probably resembled them.

However, this void did not deter my interest in hearing more about Granddaddy Simpson and uncovering the roots of his family. Even as a teenager, I garnered that there was something special about being a Reed. Sure, my last name is Collier, but I am also a Reed. I felt that being the grandson of Simpson Reed was even more honorable. Furthermore, I sensed that there was something historically mysterious about the Reed Family. I could not explain it at the time. The feeling was just there. It never went away.

Granddaddy Simpson's father was William Reed, who was affectionately known as Grandpa Bill. Mom remembered her father and aunt relaying to them that he was born into slavery in South Carolina. To the ears of a fourteen-year-old who had just seen *Roots* at school with a mild comprehension of slavery, I can clearly recall my fascination. I was too young to be sad or angry. The struggles that my enslaved ancestors endured had not fully processed in my brain. Learning about and fully comprehending African-American history was not Mississippi's strong point. Many facets of history are not highlighted in a state that many, including myself, consider as one of the most racist states in the nation. For many, unfortunately, forgetting about the past was part of life in Mississippi. Many folk felt ashamed that their ancestors were slaves – a harsh status of life that was no fault of their own. This sentiment still prevails today, not only in Mississippi but throughout America. *Let sleeping dogs lie* was the golden rule for many. However, for others in Mississippi, knowledge about the past had been so strategically swept under the rug for many decades that the events of the past were oblivious, unless one had an ancestor who was part-white or part-Native American. "We got Indian in our family" was the only fact many seemed to have held onto tightly and proudly, as it relates to their family history.

I wondered if Grandpa Bill had the same experiences as the character, Chicken George, which was famously played by actor, Ben Vereen. Although Mom was aware that her grandfather was not born in Africa, I still wondered if he was also whipped at one time for not acknowledging something like his given name. Did he have to work from sunrise to sunset, or from "can't see to can't see," on a plantation in South Carolina? How in the world did he end up in northern Mississippi? Mom's scant knowledge about her once-enslaved paternal grandfather created a spark of curiosity that would not go away. However, as a fourteen-year-old boy, uncovering more specific details about his life in slavery seemed like a very unobtainable goal. Fortunately, it was not.

This spark of curiosity about Grandpa Bill Reed remained with me throughout high school and into college. Because my parents made Canton, Mississippi their new home after graduating from college, I was not fortunate to grow up being surrounded by kin, specifically elderly family members who could tell me more about my history. This absence of extended family heightened my desire to know more. Whenever my aunt and uncles visited during the holidays, or whenever we visited them during the summers, Uncle Leon was the one to infuse Grandpa Bill Reed's name somewhere in the conversations about the past. He was the only one who was old enough to remember him. However, he failed to mention something very significant that I did not learn until the summer of 1991.

6

As if the conversation occurred yesterday, I vividly remember my aunt revealing a significant piece of family history. Aunt Eartha, who was visiting us for several days from Chicago, knew that I possessed a passion to know my family's history. Sitting on the couch, she casually shared, "Aunt John told us that Grandpa Bill's last name was not always Reed. I think it was Boyd or something, but I know that it was a name that began with a B. That was the name of the first family who owned him in South Carolina, and they sold him to a Reed Family. That's how our family got the Reed name."

This small yet large piece of family history poured more gas onto the beaming spark, now igniting a bright flame of curiosity. The desire to know more about Grandpa Bill's history was becoming overwhelming. What was the B surname? I wondered.

More gas was poured onto the burgeoning flame the following year. On the third Sunday in May of 1992, we attended Homecoming Day at Mom's home church, Beulah Baptist Church, located in a very rural area eight miles east of Como in Panola County. Attending this annual event was our ritual and a great one, indeed. Mom held on tightly to her northern Mississippi roots. Growing up in Canton, Mississippi, where everyone seemed related to each other but us, I was always excited about this annual event. Nearly everyone there was related to Mom, either on her father's side, her mother's side, or both. They even looked like family. It was not difficult to point out a Reed, and it was just as easy to point out a Davis, Mom's maternal family. Her first cousin, Armentha Reed Puryear, and Aunt Eartha could easily pass for sisters. The Homecoming Day services lasted for hours in a packed, red-bricked country church whose wooden floors created wonderful, melodic sounds as the congregation patted their feet to songs sung by the choir, including one of Cousin Rosalind Reed's famous songs, *He Promised*. Family members from as far away as Michigan would periodically come back home to attend.

This particular year was the first year of the Reed & Puryear Family Reunion. Cousin Armentha's son, Robert Earl, who everyone

7

called Bob, had traveled down from St. Louis to attend Homecoming Day and to also distribute letters to family members about the upcoming family reunion he and his mom were organizing. There had been previous "Reed Family Reunions" in the past that Cousin Armentha's brother, Cousin Enos Reed, had hosted in Benton Harbor, Michigan. We had not attended them. Therefore, the reunion letter generated an overflow of excitement. For the 1992 reunion, Cousin Bob desired to unite his mother's side of the family, the Reeds, with his father's side of the family, the Puryears. I am a Reed, and I knew that I had to be there. This will be a chance to not only meet more family members on my grandfather's side of the family, but I also wanted to know more family history.

Mom had always proclaimed that the Reed Family was very large, and that the family members at Homecoming Day were just a very small fraction of the family. Numerous relatives left Mississippi during the 50s and 60s primarily for better job opportunities in northern cities. Others left to escape from under the more ominous cloud of racism that hovered over the state.

The family reunion was slated to be held the Fourth of July weekend on Cousin Armentha's place, ten miles east of Senatobia. She and her husband, Cousin Lucious Puryear, owned property in the Looxahoma district that was part of Grandpa Bill's homestead. Everyone in the family called it the Old Home Place. During the six weeks leading up to the reunion, I envisioned hundreds of family members from Tennessee, Illinois, Ohio, Michigan, and other states gathered on the ancestral land, having a joyous time and celebrating the fact that we were part of the same bloodline. I was anxious to see if the "new" family members resembled the rest of Mom's family members who I had met at Beulah.

I was not surprised to see how family reunions became an important and necessary tradition in the Reed Family and many other African-American families. The institution of family was and continues to be one of the most important traditions among African

8

Americans. However, in order to fully comprehend the vitality of the African-American family and its importance, one must revert back to the roots – Africa. Within a small region of a massive and beautiful continent, stretching from Senegal to Angola, the ancestors were molded in culturally rich communities in which the family was the foundation of the village. Despite the diversity of traditional African societies, a cultural feature shared by nearly all of them was that life was centered around the family – often an extensive kinship network that included all who descend from a common ancestor. Interestingly, African children in the same generation were brought up more or less like sisters and brothers, rather than strictly separating themselves into siblings versus cousins.[2] Whether they hailed from the Akan culture of Ghana, the Yoruba culture of Nigeria, or the Mbundu culture of Angola, these ideologies regarding family life accompanied them to America.

Despite the physical and psychological trauma of American slavery, people of African descent held tightly onto the grave importance of family. The value and importance of family were even more amplified by the dehumanizing aspects of American slavery that allowed for the frequent dismantling of families. The importance of family was evident by the frequency of family reunions among African Americans. Dr. Ione D. Vargus, the chair of the Family Reunion Institute at Temple University, contends that African-American families participate in reunions in numbers and percentages and with consistency to which no other group of people can make claim.[3] This fact is clearly an indicator that the strength of the African legacies and the incredible resilience of its people in western society simply would not allow a complete annihilation of ancestral family values and customs to prevail.

Consequently, these ancestral values manifested on the Old Home Place. On the morning of Saturday, July 4, 1992, I awoke with a lot of excitement, as if I was a five-year-old child on Christmas morning, anxious about opening the gifts that Santa Claus had left under the

Christmas tree. This time, my gift would be the gift of extended family. This was the first family reunion that I ever attended on my mother's side of the family. My parents, sister, and I hopped in my parents' Cadillac Deville and made the two-hour journey up Interstate 55 to the Old Home Place. That two-hour car ride seemed like an all-day trip; my anticipation was building by the minute. As we pulled onto Cousin Armentha's place, I was immediately disappointed. Where were the hundreds of family members that I envisioned in my mind? Did they not know about the family reunion? Apparently, we had arrived early and were among the first attendees on the grounds. Arriving late at a function was one of my father's pet peeves; therefore, we departed Canton a little too early. Punctuality was very important to him – a trait I inherited.

Shortly after our arrival, a steady stream of family members began to pour onto the ancestral land. Some people booked hotel rooms in Memphis, Tennessee, which was forty miles away, and others opted to stay at the Howard Johnson Motel in Senatobia. Mostly the descendants of Grandpa Bill and Momma Sarah Reed populated the property, sprinkled with the descendants of Edward and Julie Puryear. Many came dressed in their navy blue and white reunion t-shirts. Slightly under one hundred people attended the grand event. Although it was not the hundreds I had envisioned, the family reunion was indeed a very momentous occasion.

Subsequent bi-annual reunions were held in Tate County up until 1998. I faithfully chaired the 1998 and 2000 reunions that were held in Memphis, Tennessee, and I co-chaired the 2004 reunion in Atlanta, Georgia with my cousin, Dr. Leroy Frazier. I was an active planning committee member for the remaining reunions – the 2002 reunion in Chicago, Illinois, the 2006 reunion in Pensacola, Florida, and the 2008 reunion in Nashville, Tennessee. The family reunions, which incorporated city bus tours, fun icebreakers, talent shows, family choirs, and more, grew to an attendance of over two hundred people, which was still a small fraction of the entire family.

"The feeling was just there."

2004 Reed & Puryear Family Reunion, Atlanta, Georgia

2006 Reed & Puryear Family Reunion, Pensacola, Florida

2008 Reed & Puryear Family Reunion, Nashville, Tennessee

As I sat on one of the benches, partaking in some scrumptious barbeque ribs and baked beans, listening to family members reminisce about their early years on the property, while others became acquainted with each other, I opened the blue family reunion book that Cousin Bob had prepared and distributed to family members. It was a treasure trove loaded with family pictures, a family tree, and even a typewritten family history. Of course, I immediately turned to the family history and read the following:

> The Reed-Puryear Family Reunion is reaching back
> from 1872 – 1992, approximately 120 years. We are
> very proud of our family history. We are going back to
> just after slavery, a period of time in United States
> history known as Reconstruction. The first Reed in our
> family after slavery was Bill Reed . . . He was born a
> slave in South Carolina around 1839. Bill was sold to a
> Reed Family of Tate County, Mississippi in the 1850's
> before the end of slavery. He remembered that his last
> name was Barr before he was sold to a Reed Family . . .
> Bill was around twenty-six years old when the Civil
> War ended.[4]

Grandpa Bill Reed's previous surname was Barr! That was the "B" surname that Aunt Eartha was trying to recall. I was ecstatic to solve this first mystery. I discovered that the surname change from Barr to Reed was common knowledge among some of the older family members. Cousin Bob had gotten the family history information from Cousin Armentha, who was one of Grandpa Bill's many granddaughters. Her father, Uncle Pleas Reed, was Granddaddy Simpson's baby brother who possessed a rather peculiar name.

After awhile, I became unsatisfied with that information. I wanted to know more – much more than what my family knew, so I thought.

Where in South Carolina did Grandpa Bill come from? What happened to his family after he was sold? Why was he sold? Did he come to Mississippi alone? What were the names of the Barr and Reed slave-owners? Did Grandpa Bill have any sisters and brothers? If so, what happened to them? A myriad of questions inundated my mind.

The following summer, on Monday, August 2, 1993, I drove to Jackson to the Mississippi Department of Archives and History (MDAH) with high hopes of uncovering more. It was only a thirty-minute drive from Canton. I was home from college for the summer and wanted to start researching my family tree before school started in three weeks. My cousin, Kwame Bandele, had recently given me a dose of encouragement and research tips to begin the journey. He had traced his family back six generations. Not knowing exactly where and how to start, the archivist at the MDAH suggested that I view the U. S. Federal Census records first. She was a very nice lady who willingly gave a curious twenty-year-old a crash course in understanding the soundex and viewing the microfilmed census records. Undoubtedly, she was surprised to see a youngster interested in genealogy, especially an African-American one. The staff at the Archives, especially the one in Mississippi, was accustomed to having many older white patrons. I was a rarity.

I was anxious to learn more about all of my ancestors, but I decided to start my research with the Reeds. Grandpa Bill's story intrigued me the most. With the archivist's assistance, I first loaded the 1920 soundex and then the 1920 U. S. Federal Census onto the microfilm reader. I was so excited that I initially had difficulty with the microfilm reader. At that time, the 1920 census was the latest census available. The 1930 U. S. Federal Census was not released for public viewing until 2002. All censuses are held for seventy-two years before their release. Supposedly, seventy-two years was chosen as the time restriction because it was the average lifespan of Americans. After scrolling down the entries of many Reed, Reid, or Read families in Mississippi in 1920, I finally came upon my family in Tate County.

Grandpa Bill was the head of household, and South Carolina was recorded as his birthplace, as oral history had proclaimed.

"This is him!" I said loudly with excitement. I felt the other patrons' eyes glancing over at me after my loud outburst, but I did not care. I was in genealogy heaven. I then retrieved the actual 1920 census sheet on which the family was recorded in order to gather more information that was not included on the soundex card.

In 1920, Grandpa Bill, his wife, my great-grandmother Sarah, who was sixty-eight and my grandfather, a thirty-nine-year-old bachelor, were the only three people in the household. Granddaddy Simpson married his first wife, Addie Person, three years later, with whom he had Uncle Leon. Addie died in childbirth in 1931, giving birth to their son, Thomas Adison; little Thomas died seven months later from a whooping cough. Mom had already shared that her paternal grandmother's name was Sarah Partee Reed. Sarah had also died before she was born, but Mom referred to her as "Momma Sarah," as if she had known her well. As I studied the census sheet, tracing the house-to-house march of the census-taker who walked through the rural Tate County community with his census book, I immediately noticed that Grandpa Bill's next-door neighbors were his children and grandchildren. I was already familiar with some of their names from my Mom and her siblings' conversations about the past.

On the Old Home Place, Grand-uncle Dock Reed, whose real name was Doctor Rogers Reed, headed a household that contained his wife Mary Frances and their eleven children. Grand-uncle Jimmy Reed, who was the oldest, headed a household that contained his wife, Anna Davis, and their five teenage children. Interestingly, Aunt Anna was my maternal grandmother's aunt, and Aunt Mary Frances was my maternal grandmother's second cousin. In addition, Granddaddy Simpson's older brother, Uncle Willie Reed, was also married to my grandmother's second cousin, also named Mary, with whom he had five sons. Many of Mom's paternal first cousins were also her maternal cousins. This explained why many people in the Reed Family looked alike.

Living on the ancestral land also were Grand-uncle Pleas Reed, his wife Aristarcus Pratcher, and their three young children. After 1920, Uncle Pleas, whose official name was Pleasant, and Aunt Aristarcus, whose name derived from the Bible, had eight additional children. Living besides Uncle Pleas was my great-grandparents' youngest daughter, Grand-aunt Martha Jane, who was in a household with her husband, Ollie Deberry, and their five young children. They later had six additional children.

The 1920 U. S. Federal Census allowed me to paint a mental picture of the Old Home Place. Closely mimicking an African village, forty family members were clustered there on the ancestral land. On January 12, 1920, the day the census-taker visited, Grandpa Bill and Momma Sarah Reed were surrounded by five of their eleven children and twenty-four of their fifty-seven grandchildren. Additionally, four of Momma Sarah's nephews, Claimus, Jack, Dempsey, and Square Partee Jr., as well as a niece, Druella Partee, were also on the place. Mom has very fond memories of Cousin Jack Partee, a jolly and obese cousin who lived with them for awhile. Unquestionably, the societal codes regarding family life in West Africa accompanied the enslaved ancestors to America and were still prevailing decades after the end of slavery, even on the Old Home Place.

Grand-uncle Willie Reed and Grand-aunt Mary Reed Lee resided in nearby Panola County with their families, and Grand-aunt John Ella lived in Memphis, Tennessee with her husband, Eli Bobo. Uncle Eli Bobo, along with the aforementioned spouses, was also my maternal grandmother's cousin. In the 1930s, Aunt John moved back on the Old Home Place after the death of her second husband, John Green, who was discovered to be a con artist. He left her penniless after a very short-term marriage. Granddaddy Simpson and his brothers built her a quaint home just a "shouting distance" away. Mom remembered, "Aunt John didn't have any children, but she loved for us to come visit her every day if my mother permitted us to. Sometimes, Mom didn't seem thrilled about some of the conversations she would have with my sister and me. She loved to tease us about getting a boyfriend and husband. We were only in our early teens and Mom felt that her conversations should have been that of encouraging us to do our best in school and perhaps going to college." Apparently, some of those conversations also involved the history of the family that Mom and Aunt Eartha had recalled.

Despite the harsh racial climate of the time, growing up on the Old Home Place were great memories for Mom and her siblings. She shared, "Life back then was different from what children experience today. We always had what we needed, but not a lot of surplus to waste because my parents believed in sharing with the neighbors or anyone who needed a lift." The rural community of Looxahoma was a self-sustaining, farming community where everyone continuously provided moral, emotional, psychological, and economic support to its residents. People shared traditional values of hard work, family life, and a dedication to the church. Men, women, and children all worked diligently to support the family farms. Mom proudly reminisced:

"Living on the farm afforded me many opportunities to gain experiences in work ethics, doing such as we could to help my father on the farm harvesting cotton, peas, corn, potatoes, peanuts, etc. My sister and I got great joy going to the sorghum mill and watching my father tend his mill, making molasses for himself and other neighbors and friends. Most of the times, he was too busy to go home to get lunch, so my sister and I would carry his lunch to him. The house that we lived in had six rooms with a fireplace and several wood burning heaters to keep us warm in the winter. During the winter, my parents would roast sweet potatoes in the ashes in the fireplace and cook peanuts and popcorn over the fire. Most of our food items were raised on our farm. Only a few

The children of Bill & Sarah Reed (left to right): Jimmy Reed (1872-1959), John Ella Reed Bobo (1882-1974), and Pleasant "Pleas" Reed (1888-1966). The picture was taken on the Old Home Place in the 1950s. (From the collection of Robert Puryear)

food items had to be purchased in a store.  My siblings and I had several cows to milk and after which my mother would have us churn the milk and that was the butter we used.  Horses, cows, hogs, and chicken were all raised there on the farm.  My father took pride in his fruit orchards where he grew peaches, plums, pears, watermelons, and figs.  There was always plenty of food to go around to his family and share with neighbors and friends.  On Saturdays, my parents would take us to Senatobia to shop and they would allow time for us to go to the theatre, as we called 'show' back then."

Fortunately, I located Grandpa Bill Reed in the 1910 and 1900 U. S. Federal Censuses.  In 1920, his reported age was seventy-one, placing his birth year around 1849.  In 1910, his reported age was sixty-four, thereby placing his birth year around 1846.  Also, the 1900 census-taker recorded September 1846 as his birth month and year.  Many former slaves did not know their date and year of birth.  Consequently, census-takers often calculated their birth years by them relating their time of birth to historical events, like the beginning or the end of Civil War or when they were emancipated.  Levi Ashley of Amite County, Mississippi relayed, "I don't know how old I is, but I was tol' I was nine year old when I was sot free. Yes-sum, I 'member a heap 'bout de War."[5]  Based on the federal census reports, there was reasonable certainty that Grandpa Bill Reed was born in or around the year 1846, instead of the year 1839.  I was the great-grandson of a man who was around nineteen years old when he became a free man after the Civil War ended.

Since the 1870 U. S. Federal Census was recorded just five years after the end of slavery, it is vitally important for African-American genealogy research.  That census was very often the first official record that recorded former slaves by their first and last names, giving them some well-deserved respect and dignity.  Someone named Bill Reed was living in Panola County in 1870.  The Tate/Panola County line was the southern boundary of the Old Home Place. He was reported as being sixteen years old and was living in the household of Glasgow Wilson. Was this Grandpa Bill? I was not sure since my great-grandfather was actually around twenty-four years old in 1870.

After I viewed the census records, the archivist advised me to also view marriage records, as well as other sources there at the MDAH. With only a little time remaining before the MDAH closed for the day, I viewed the marriage records for DeSoto and Panola County, Mississippi. Prior to 1873, Tate County was a part of DeSoto County. Luckily, I found Grandpa Bill's marriage license of his marriage to Momma Sarah Partee. Glasgow Wilson was the minister who had married them on November 8, 1871 in Panola County. Therefore, he was likely the same Bill Reed reported in his household the previous year.

Cousin Bob's write-up in the 1992 family reunion book noted that Grandpa Bill was sold to a Reed Family in Tate County, Mississippi in the 1850s. I had recently read more books about African-American genealogy and had gained some knowledge about tracking down the last slave-owner. Several sources advised researchers to view the 1850 and 1860 U. S. Federal Slave Schedules to possibly determine the name of the last enslaver. Slave schedules are censuses that contain the slave-owners' names and the age, sex, and color of each of their slaves. Columns also report the number of fugitive and manumitted slaves. There is also a column that noted slaves who were deaf, blind, insane, or idiotic. Unfortunately, very few names of slaves were recorded. First names were only recorded for those who were 100 years old or older. Many former slaves took the surname of their last enslaver, while many of them chose another surname. Apparently, Grandpa Bill opted to retain his last enslaver's surname, and I wanted to know the name of that Reed slave-owner. It was a vital piece of family history. Obtaining that information was my main goal during my next trip to the Archives the next day.

Since Reed was a common surname, I anticipated it being a laborious task to positively identify Grandpa Bill's last enslaver. His profile in 1860 would have been a Black male who was around thirteen or fourteen years old. That year, a man named J. A. Reed had five slaves – three males, ages 45, 4, and 1. Sam Houston Reed had seven slaves – three males, ages 33, 4, and 3. Zalmon Reed had eight slaves – three males, ages 25, 8, and 2. E. T. Reed had eight slaves – five males, ages 16, 8, 6, 6, and 4. J. B. Reed had four slaves – two males, ages 25 and 3. Of those five possibilities, E. T. Reed was the only possible candidate since he owned a sixteen-year-old male. The 1860 U. S. Federal Census revealed that he was a seventeen-year-old student living in the household of fifty-two-year-old Sam Houston Reed, who was probably his father. Although he was rather young, E. T. Reed was reported as having a personal estate valued at $8,750 and a real estate valued at $3,000. This was evidence that he was the same person reported in the slave schedule since slaves were considered "property" and were of monetary value. Also, Sam Houston and E. T. Reed lived in the Looxahoma district, which is the same district where the Old Home Place was located.

I had learned that it was common for former slaves to settle within a short distance from their last enslavers. By 1870, many still lived on the farms and plantations where they had been enslaved, but they were now employed as laborers and sharecroppers. Being nominally free, African Americans had emerged out of slavery with little to no adequate means of self-support in a largely agricultural society. Would I be able to confirm if the small farm of Sam Houston Reed was where Grandpa Bill lived his last days in slavery? I was hopeful.

School started several weeks later, and I entered my junior year at Mississippi State University, majoring in Civil Engineering. Although a love of history had developed, I remained in this technical field mainly because of the nice salaries engineers are paid after college. Also, I knew that changing my major during my junior year, from engineering to a history-related field, would not sit very well with my parents. They had sacrificed much so that my sister and I could attend college. It essentially meant starting over. School was now a priority, and my research had to take a back seat for awhile. However, it did not take a back seat in my mind. I often sat in classes wondering about Grandpa Bill's life as a slave, possibly on Sam Houston Reed's farm. In retrospect, I wonder how I was able to complete my requirements to receive my engineering degree when my mind had become so thirsty for African-American history. Undoubtedly, it was because of the grace of God.

Several months later, on Friday night, April 22, 1994, I decided to relax in my dorm room rather than going out to a party or playing cards with friends. Genealogy had such a hold on me that I wanted to spend that night on the computer, reading messages and research tips posted to the African-American genealogy message boards on America Online. It became my home away from home. That night, I posted the following:

Hello, I am a newcomer to America Online and was elated to see the African-American Genealogy section. I am currently in the process of tracing my maternal family roots. My mother's father was Simpson Reed, born in 1881 in Tate County, Mississippi. Simpson's father was Bill Reed. My great-grandfather Bill was born a slave in South Carolina around 1846. According to oral history, he told his family that his last name was Barr when he was a slave in S.C. Bill was brought to Mississippi during the 1850s. He became a slave for a Reed Family in Tate County, Mississippi (it was DeSoto County prior to 1873). . . . I recently visited the MS Dept. of Archives and found several persons in the 1860 slave schedule for DeSoto County with the surname Reed who owned slaves, but I had no way of knowing for sure who was truly the slave-owner. Any advice on how to pinpoint the name of my great-grandfather's slave owners in Mississippi and in South Carolina will be greatly appreciated.

A week later, on Saturday morning, April 30, 1994, I woke up to a sunny day in Starkville, Mississippi. I had decided not to go home for the weekend, which was a two-hour drive from campus, and remained in my dorm room to prepare for my final exams. As I typically do in the mornings, I logged onto America Online to see if I had received any emails. I had one message with the subject, "Researching Family Roots," from Angela Walton-Raji. I had seen her name before. She was a well-known African-American genealogist. She was also the manager and moderator of the African-American Special Interest Group in the Genealogy Forum on America Online. Angela was responding to my post from the previous week. She typed the following:

> I found your post interesting! My mother's great-
> grandmother lived in Tippah County, Mississippi. After the
> Civil War, her husband had died fighting with one of the
> Black regiments in Tennessee. Subsequently, she had several
> children and remarried a man by the name of Pleasant Barr
> who was originally from South Carolina. She did have one
> child with Barr, Elijah. Pleasant Barr died in the late 1880s
> and Amanda eventually moved to Memphis, Tennessee. I
> have lots of information about Amanda's line, and virtually
> no information about the Barr line. I am curious if this Barr
> might be related to your Barr from South Carolina. I would
> be willing to do some work to identify the slave-owner of this
> Barr also. Please share more info. Also, welcome to the
> African American section. Several of us meet online to chat
> live on Tuesdays at 9 PM EST. I hope you can join us then. I
> hope to hear from you soon.[6]

I was so stunned by her message that I immediately read it to my roommate, Derrick Pate, who also shared an interest in genealogy but not the type of obsession that I carried. Very few folk like me had that type of obsession. I found Angela's message to be extremely interesting and amazing, to say the least. Grandpa Bill's youngest son was also named Pleasant, but everyone simply called him Pleas. Mom talked about Uncle Pleas Reed so often, frequently recalling his jovial, lively personality, that I ascertained that he was her favorite uncle. Was Pleasant Barr a relative? Could it be sheer coincidence that the unusual name Pleasant and the surname Barr, with ties to South Carolina, were in both of our family histories? I immediately printed her message on my dot matrix printer and stored it in my research folder. There had to be some kind of connection. The feeling was just there.

The next month, I completed my junior year at Mississippi State with fair grades. My grades would have been better if I had not been so consumed with genealogy research and obsessed with determining how I was going to break down this brick wall of identifying Grandpa Bill Reed's last enslaver and possibly tracing him back to South Carolina. My obsession became so strong that I often prayed to God at night for His guidance in helping me to uncover Grandpa Bill's origins. I desperately wanted to know where in South Carolina he had been enslaved.

Shortly after arriving home for the summer, I spent more time at the Archives. This time, I planned to research my father's family and my mother's maternal family since I had reached a brick wall in my Reed research. My father was thrilled because I spent so much time on my mother's paternal family, and he was curious about the things that can be uncovered about his family roots. He and Mom were amazed at the availability of records and the stories they told. Little did I know that my genealogy shovel would dig much deeper into my family's mysterious past.

*Left to right: My mother, Versia Reed Collier, and her sister, Eartha Reed Campbell, the daughters of Simpson & Minnie Reed and the youngest granddaughters of Bill & Sarah Reed's 57 grandchildren.*

*Doctor Rogers "Dock" (1878 – 1958)*
*& Mary Reed*

*Martha Jane Reed Deberry*
*(1892 – 1971)*

# *Chapter 2*

## "What a great griot he was!"

he second bi-annual Reed & Puryear Family Reunion was planned for the first weekend in July 1994, with a picnic to be held on the Old Home Place on Saturday afternoon. This time, I was determined to break further out of my shell and talk with more of my older relatives about Grandpa Bill Reed. I failed to conduct interviews at the first family reunion since the information in the reunion book had provided me with new information. Digging deeper into Grandpa Bill's mysterious past had now become a burgeoning desire.

One of the older relatives in attendance was Mom's first cousin, Isaac Deberry Sr., who was simply called "Cut'n Ike." "Cut'n" is the southern slang for cousin. He was seventy-nine years old, and the second of eleven children born to Granddaddy Simpson's baby sister, Aunt Martha Jane Deberry.

As a shy young man, I walked up to him nervously and introduced myself, "Hello Cousin Ike. I'm Melvin, your Uncle Simpson's daughter's son."

*Isaac "Ike" Deberry Sr., the grandson of Bill & Sarah Reed. In this picture, he is relaying family history about Bill Reed at the 2004 Reed & Puryear Family Reunion.*

He asked curiously, "You Sister's boy or Versie Lee's boy?"

Since Aunt Eartha was the oldest daughter, she was called "Sister" by many of the older relatives. This was common among many African-American families, and this naming practice can be traced back to Africa.

"I'm Versie's son," I replied. Hearing my relatives refer to Mom as "Versie Lee" was rather humorous. Mom rarely told anyone her middle name.

Cousin Ike acknowledged, "You know Uncle Simp was my favorite uncle!"

I was not surprised by this statement, considering how Mom and her siblings esteemed their father. She later shared how my grandfather helped his baby sister Martha Jane with her eleven kids after her husband died. In many ways, my grandfather became a father figure to his fatherless nieces and nephews.

Eager to change the subject to Grandpa Bill, I commented with more confidence, "Cut'n Ike, I have been doing some research on Grandpa Bill. I read in the last reunion book how a Barr family in South Carolina had sold him to a Reed Family in Tate County."

Cousin Ike nodded and said emphatically, "No, that ain't right! He was already free when he got to Mississippi. He told me it was around 1866 or '67, I believe, when they came here."

I was startled.

Having the mental ability to recall the approximate year his grandfather migrated to Mississippi from South Carolina, an event that occurred decades before his birth, was a mouth dropper. I soon ascertained that Cousin Ike was a living history book or a griot. In the annals of African history, a griot, pronounced *gree-oh,* was the honored member of the village who was the knowledgeable storyteller entrusted with the pivotal task of relaying the history of a family, ethnic group, or village. This definition perfectly described the important role in the Reed Family that Cousin Ike was bestowed. What a great griot he was!

"Oh, really?" I said with amazement. "He was never a slave here in Mississippi?" I asked, wondering if the time I had spent at the MDAH researching the 1860 DeSoto County Slave Schedule was in vain.

Cousin Ike remarked coolly, "Oh, no. Grandpa and his sister, who was Cut'n Louvenia Hunter's momma, and some more other folks, came here on a wagon train that were pulled by mules shortly after they got freed. He told me that some man from Mississippi came to South Carolina and told them that Mississippi was the land of milk and honey with fat pigs running around with apples in their mouths. They were still living so poorly like slaves on the Reed man's place that some of them decided to follow this man back here to Mississippi."

With anxious ears and a happy soul, I continued listening as if my life depended on his words.

He further relayed, "Grandpa would sit under his sycamore tree and tell us 'bout dem slavery days before he died.  He died in '37, shortly after Thanksgiving.  He went out to chop some firewood, and it was raining that day, and he came down with pneumonia.  He had chopped three or four loads, too.  That was a strong ole man.  He died about two or three days later.  I don't think he made it to 100, but he wasn't far from it.  I was a grown man and married at the time.  Momma had moved back on Grandpa's place with all of us eleven kids after my Daddy died in '27.  I was with Grandpa on the place from that time up until he died.  I sure do miss that ole man."

I continued to pry for more information. "Did he tell you the name of the slave-owner," I asked.

Cousin Ike thought for a minute.  Then, he expressed, "Oh, yeah.  He called that man's name out so many times."

After pausing for another minute to think, he continued, "Wait.  I think Grandpa called him Masser Lem Reed or something like that.  I can't recall the name of the Barr man who first owned him.  The Barrs had sold him to Lem Reed when he was a boy.  He talked about that all the time."

I was stunned.

Cousin Ike continued, "He remembered how Lem Reed was saying that he was old enough to be a good plow boy on his place, so he must have been around ten, eleven, or twelve, I reckon, when he was sold to him.  He would always talk about how he would ride with the Reed man over the pasture.  He had a saddling horse and he'll put Grandpa Bill up behind him to open the gates for 'em."

Cousin Ike further shared, "Grandpa told me that on the day they got freed, Lem Reed came out on his porch and called all the slaves up to the house and said to them, 'Y'all are as free as I am.'  He asked them to stay on the place to help him bring in the crop and he promised to pay them.  Grandpa said that they stayed for a lil while and then they decided to follow this man to Mississippi to make a better living for themselves. Hearing that there were fat pigs running around with apples in their mouths got them all excited."

Cousin Ike chuckled softly, knowing that this anonymous man had used exaggerated tales to coerce them to come back to Mississippi with him.

"Traveling from South Carolina to Mississippi by mules and wagons must have been a really long journey," I commented.

My statement sparked even more recollections. Cousin Ike responded with certainty, "Yes, it was! He told me that he walked most of the way, alongside the wagons. He would tell me how they would travel about twenty or thirty miles a day. It took them around a month or so to get here. I remember him telling us how someone had died while they were coming through Alabama, and they dug a grave and buried him there. I can't remember if it was a family member or not that had died."

"Where did they live when they got to Mississippi?" I asked.

By this point, I was not as interested in meeting "new" cousins who attended this family reunion and becoming reacquainted with others. Cousin Ike's memories were enthralling. I was a sponge who wanted to sit and soak up all of the wonderful family history from someone who obviously had a very close relationship with the former slave and who clearly had a better memory of his stories.

Cousin Ike answered, "Grandpa told me that when they got here, they worked for Mr. Sam Lyles, on the Lyles Place down in Panola County. He used to tell me how they had to clear a whole lot of land down there, and they hardly made any money. Whatever he made, he must have saved it because somehow, he was able to buy all of this land and farm for himself. Grandpa had over three hundred acres right here, ya know. He couldn't read and write but he sure was a smart man. And the house he and Grandma stayed in was a fairly nice house for Black folks back then. It had a kitchen, a living room, four large bedrooms that was divided by a big hallway. They had a piano in the hallway. The grandchil'ren played on it but if Grandpa or

Grandma heard you playin' that Blues music on it, you was in a heap of trouble. You could only play church music on it."

"Grandpa Bill was a church-going man?"

"Oh, yeah. He was a faithful member of Bulow (Beulah) until he died. He used to tell us about the day he got his religion. He and some of his buddies were gambling under a tree one Sunday. Well, he said that Momma Sarah was on her way to church. They weren't married at the time. She was riding in the back of Uncle Square Partee's wagon, and she spotted Grandpa and his friends. Well, she ordered her brother to ride passed them so she can speak her mind about him disrespecting the Lord's Day. When she got Grandpa's attention, she told him, 'Watch me you sinner man as I go to worship the Lord.' Grandpa said that he felt so bad that he started going to church."

Cousin Ike chuckled. "It was shortly before he and Momma Sarah married and not long after he got here from South Carolina."

I then inquired with anticipation, "Did he ever mention where in South Carolina they came from?"

Cousin Ike replied, "Oh, yeah. He called that place out so many times, but I sure can't think of the name of the town right now."

He paused for a minute to think, and then expressed, "Maybe it'll come to me soon but I don't remember it right now." I was disappointed.

Cousin Ike was thrilled to know that I was interested in tracing our family roots. His sharp memory impressed me beyond words. He urged me to keep in contact with him. He would say ardently, "Let me know what you dig up!"

This conversation with him was the first of many conversations, visits, and phone calls. He had the keys of knowledge to unlock the gateway to the past that few of my other elderly relatives had possessed. Even when I had gained the courage to telephone other relatives to see what they remembered, such as another grandson, Cousin Enos Reed, I was often instructed, "Talk to Cut'n Ike. He will probably remember a lot more than I can." Their declaration was an understatement, indeed.

A few weeks after the reunion, I called Cousin Ike again to pique his brain further. I had more questions to ask after digesting the goldmine of information he had given me at the reunion. Also, I had recently visited the Archives and found Grandpa Bill's sister in the census. She was Mary Pratt, the wife of David Pratt, and South Carolina was also reported as their birthplace. The Pratts resided nearby in Panola County. According to the census, Aunt Mary was born around 1850, and she had three children, Louvenia, Sue, and William. Mom remembered Cousin Louvenia's son, Simon Hunter, who was over seven feet tall and who was a big land-owner in Panola County near Hunters Chapel Church, a church named after the family. She never knew exactly how Simon was her cousin until now.

Mom recalled, "When I was small, he would come to Beulah sometimes, and I would ask Daddy, 'Who is that real tall man?' Daddy would say, 'He's your cousin.'"

On the phone, I proclaimed, "Cousin Ike, I found Grandpa Bill's sister, Mary. She was a few years younger than him."

He replied, "Yeah, that sure was her name. She died before I came along but Momma always told me that Cut'n Louvenia was her first cousin because her mother was Grandpa Bill's sister."

"Did he have other siblings?"

He revealed, "Yes. He talked about a bunch of family he had when he was in South Carolina, but I guess no one knows whatever happened to them. You know, he told me that he had an older brother who got sold away. He said that his big brother was a hard worker, and he could cut a load of firewood in a real short time. Then, one day, a speculator came on the place, saw how good of a worker he was, and offered the boss man some money to buy him. Well, the boss man took the offer and sold Grandpa's brother. He said he never saw his brother no more after that."

"Do you remember his brother's name?" I asked.

"No, I'm sure he told me, but I can't remember." Cousin Ike further recollected, "He also told me that he had a sister who took care of him. I think it was another sister who was older than him and Cut'n Louvenia's mother. I don't know if they were on the Barr place or the Reed place, but he used to tell us how the overseer had whipped his sister one day. I don't remember what for. He said that he got so angry that he vowed to kill that man when he grew up. He didn't like for nobody messin' with his big sister. I wonder what became of her?"

In wonderment, Cousin Ike continued, "You know, they had some hard times back in dem slavery days. Grandpa would tell me how he was the water boy, and how he had to carry buckets of water to the other slaves in the field. He had to carry the boss man some water first, and then he had to go and refill the buckets and take them out to the fields so the slaves could have something to drink while they worked."

To verify if Grandpa Bill Reed was truly still in South Carolina during the Civil War, I asked, "Grandpa was a teenager when the Civil War broke out, did he talk about the War?"

He replied confidently, "Oh, yes! He told me how he used to hear the guns going off near the place. He was on the Reed place when the War was going on because he told me that one day, Lem Reed came and got him and they went walking with a shovel. For some reason, he said the boss man trusted him over the other slaves. Well, they walked to the top of a hill, and Lem had him to dig a big hole. He had a sack full of gold, and he was afraid that the soldiers would come on the place and steal it, so they buried it on top of a hill. Grandpa always used to say that if he could get back to South Carolina, he could find the spot where they buried that gold."

Since Grandpa Bill was living with a man named Glasgow Wilson in 1870, I questioned, "Have you ever heard of a man named Glasgow Wilson?"

His response surprised me. "That man was some kin to Grandpa. I don't know how but they were close kin. He talked about him often, and I think he was with the group that came to Mississippi with them.

I don't remember ever laying eyes on him, but that strange name, Glasco, was always in his stories."

The 1880 U. S. Federal Census of Tate County confirmed that Glasgow Wilson and his wife Rachel were born in South Carolina. Interestingly, his oldest daughter Leah, reported as eighteen years old, was also born in South Carolina, while his next child, a ten-year-old son named Robert, was born in Mississippi. This confirmed that the migration to Mississippi had occurred during the 1860s, after 1862 and before 1870. That census also reported that Glasgow was a preacher.

Cousin Ike and I talked so often about Grandpa Bill, and had developed such a close relationship, that I began to see myself as more than just his first cousin-once removed. He became a surrogate grandfather. He had been a single father of ten children whom he raised alone after the untimely demise of his wife, Essie Kay. At the age of seventy-nine, he now had a passel of grandchildren and great-grandchildren, and I felt a part of that family lot that contained well over fifty people. Cousin Ike continued to share how Grandpa Bill would sit under his sycamore tree and tell his grandchildren about his early life in South Carolina. He found the stories to be quite fascinating, as well as heart-breaking, and many of the stories were still stuck in his mind many years later.

Shortly after moving to Memphis, Tennessee in 1996, my cousins, Wallace Reed, Dr. Leroy Frazier, and I drove down to Senatobia to visit with Cousin Ike. He lived about eight miles west of Senatobia with his companion, Gladys Alexander. We wanted him to show us the exact spot where Grandpa Bill's house was located on the Old Home Place, so we all headed out to the ancestral land. When we arrived at Cousin Armentha's house, we all hopped into her Lincoln Continental, and she drove us down into the pasture, directly behind her house. She handled that car like a pro down a very bumpy, dirt roadway in the middle of a field until we approached a wooded area where a car could not be driven. We exited the car and proceeded to follow Cousin Ike. He had spotted the old roadway that once led to Grandpa Bill's house, which was now eroded and overgrown in weeds and bushes. My cousin, James Hibbler, had forewarned that the area may be haunted with spirits, but we were not afraid. If the spirits were of Grandpa Bill, Granddaddy Simpson, or even Great-uncle Jimmy Reed, who was Cousin Wallace's grandfather and Cousin Leroy's great-grandfather, I knew that they would not do any harm to us, their offspring.

We finally reached a point where Cousin Ike was certain that we were standing where the old home was located. He looked around in wonderment, and then he spotted the remnants from the old sycamore tree. "That's got to be from that old tree," he said enthusiastically, pointing to young tree full of healthy green leaves. He had not been there in over fifty years. He was clearly moved.

"Me and Grandpa spent many days under that old tree. I would love to hear him talk about them old times. His stories always fascinated me because I didn't know that folks actually went through the things he had to go through, but he talked about it with us," Cousin Ike expressed.

With teary eyes and a touched soul, Cousin Ike began to sing the following verses of an old Negro spiritual:

> *May the works that I've done speak for me.*
> *May the works that I've done speak for me.*
> *When I'm resting in my grave,*
> *There's nothing more to be said.*
> *May the works I've done speak for me.*
> *May the life I live speak for me.*
> *May the life I live speak for me.*
> *When I'm resting in my grave,*
> *There's nothing more to be said.*
> *May the life I live speak for me.*

Despite his tribulations, Grandpa Bill Reed was obviously not a tight-lipped man, but one who believed that his children and grandchildren should know their history, the good and the not-so-good. Symbolic of the Sankofa bird, an African icon that has its feet firmly planted forward while its head is looking back, he clearly believed that we must reach back and reclaim our past so we can move forward, understanding why and how we came to be who we are today. He understood who he was as an African-American man, never forgot the struggles that he endured as a slave during the first nineteen years of his life, and was determined to make a better life for him and his family. Like Cousin Ike expressed, Grandpa Bill was indeed a remarkable, strong man. Finding him has made me stronger. His willingness to share his history and Cousin Ike's incredible remembrance of those stories would soon unearth and confirm more happenings of the past that I would had never imagined.

The now-eroded and overgrown roadway that led up to Grandpa Bill Reed's house on his 300-plus-acre farm he purchased shortly after migrating to Mississippi as a free young man from South Carolina. His farm is known as the Old Home Place, Tate County, Mississippi.

Isaac (Ike) Deberry and Armentha Reed Puryear
Standing by the remnants of that old sycamore tree
Grandchildren of Bill & Sarah Reed

*In May 2004, descendants of Bill & Sarah Reed purchased and dedicated a 7-feet tall monument that was placed at their graveside at Beulah Baptist Church Cemetery, Como, Mississippi.*

*Pleasant "Pleas" Reed (1888 – 1966), the youngest son of Bill & Sarah Reed
(From the collection of Robert Puryear)*

*My maternal grandmother, Minnie Davis Reed (1908 – 1971),
the wife of Simpson Reed*

# *Chapter 3*

## Gone but not forgotten.

*G*oing back into the past and uncovering my ancestors' story had now become an addiction, and I did not desire any form of rehabilitation whatsoever. This became a welcomed outlet and my favorite hobby which kept me in a state of wonderment about the lives that my ancestors lived and the mountains and molehills that they had to climb in order for me to get to where I am now. I felt as if I was the only young person in his early twenties who was even remotely interested in history and genealogy research. I'd talk to some – not all – of my friends about my research, but I knew to keep the conversations short. Other than my family, no one really cared that I was the great-grandson of slaves. No one cared that some of my maternal roots went beyond northern Mississippi but back to somewhere in South Carolina. No one cared that much of my paternal roots actually began in North Carolina rather than in Leake and Warren County, Mississippi. The interest among my peers was just not there. My only refuge to totally dwell in a world where there were people who understood the genealogical spell that I was under was on the Internet, which was growing by the minute. This world kept me inspired to continue further into my ancestral past.

Death certificates have helped many people to dig deeper into their ancestral past. Those records provide the father's name, the mother's maiden name, birthplaces of the recently deceased and the parents, the date of death, the place of burial, and the cause of death. I compiled a list of ancestors whose death certificates I wanted to find. Of course, Grandpa Bill Reed was at the top of the list. Cousin Ike Deberry had already informed me that he died in 1937, shortly after Thanksgiving. Therefore, I was armed with a death date to aid the search.

Since the Mississippi death certificates that are housed at the MDAH cover the years 1912 to 1943, I was anxious to see if there was one for him. Uncovering the names of his parents, if the informant possessed that knowledge, would be a huge milestone. Cousin Ike's astonishing memories had conveyed Grandpa Bill and his sister's migration to Mississippi shortly after the Civil War, without any mention thus far of their parents. Perhaps, his death certificate may open another door to the past.

I checked the Mississippi death index microfilm for the year 1937. To my sheer delight, Grandpa Bill was listed. I recorded the death year and death certificate number to give to the archivist for the correct microfiche. She soon handed me the microfiche, and I proceeded expeditiously to a microfiche reader in the back of the dimly lit microfilm room. I could hear drum rolls beating in my head as I loaded the microfiche onto the reader, hoping to knock down a major brick wall. Would this document tell me where in South Carolina Grandpa Bill was born? Would I find out the names of his parents? My anxiety level was rapidly reaching its peak as I nervously sought for death certificate #23767.

Several minutes later, I located the revealing certificate. At the top, Looxahoma was recorded as the district of residence in Tate County. "Yes, this is him," I commented to myself. I then directed my eyes down to the line where the father's name was to be written. The name "Ples Barr" was recorded. His birthplace was recorded as being South Carolina. The informant was Uncle Jimmy Reed.

"Wow," I said ecstatically. "Grandpa Bill's father's name was Pleas Barr! He had named Uncle Pleas Reed after his father," I openly commented to myself, since I was alone in the microfilm room.

The discovery left me so taken aback that I sat there in my chair and starred at the certificate for several minutes. It was a crucial document. If anyone had noticed the expression on my face, they would have believed that I had just seen a ghost. I instantly thought about the e-mail that I received from Angela Walton-Raji two years earlier. Was her Pleasant Barr my great-great-grandfather?

*Bill Reed's death certificate identified his father as "Ples Barr."*

The death certificate revealed that Grandpa Bill died on November 31, 1937, nearly ten months before Mom was born. Cousin Ike was very accurate in remembering the time of his death. Uncle Jimmy reported his age as ninety years and four months; therefore, he believed that his birth occurred in South Carolina in July 1847. The cause of death was noted as "acute cold and senility." According to Cousin Ike, Grandpa Bill had been out chopping wood in the cold rain several days before his demise, and he had contracted what he thought was pneumonia.

Unfortunately, in the line where the mother's name was to be written, the words, "not known," were written instead. Ditto marks were written in the spot that asked for her birthplace. Uncle Jimmy apparently lacked knowledge of his paternal grandmother and her birthplace. I was disappointed.

After leaving the Archives, I rushed home to e-mail Angela about this huge discovery. Excitedly, she e-mailed the following response several hours later:

This is absolutely amazing! I suspect that we might have one and the same Pleas. I can tell you a little bit about him. He married Amanda Young after the Civil War, in Ripley, Mississippi. I don't know how they met. She was married to my great-great-grandfather, Berry Young, before the War. Her son and husband died in the War, and she then remarried to Pleasant Barr. They had one son, Elijah Barr. The family later moved to Memphis, and Elijah married there. I don't know what happened to his family, although some are believed to still be in Tennessee. Pleasant Barr was a mature man at the time that he and Amanda married, and he died in the late 1880s. I found this out on the military pension file that Amanda filed to receive a widow's pension from her first husband's death. She had to give lots of information in that process . . . I have wanted to learn more about the origins of

42

Pleasant Barr. He was my great-great-grandmother's husband, and they had a child together, whose descendants would be both of our cousins! Since he and Amanda were married for quite some time, his presence in my family cannot be ignored. Where is Tate County in relation to Tippah County? I will be more interested in learning more about whether this is the same Pleas . . . This is great news! I hope we have the same man![1]

I began to investigate Pleasant Barr of Tippah County to see if he could positively be Grandpa Bill's father. Per the census records, he was the only man with that first and last name in the South. Based on his reported age in the 1880 U. S. Federal Census, he was born in South Carolina around 1814. Pleasant, Amanda, and their son, Elijah, were the only Barrs, black or white, in Tippah County. He was about thirty-two years older than Grandpa Bill, definitely of age to be his father. But, was he?

Perhaps, Pleasant Barr chose to take the Barr surname after Emancipation because his first enslaver in South Carolina was a Barr, possibly the same person who sold Grandpa Bill to Lem Reed. I had learned from various sources that many former slaves chose the surname of a previous enslaver who owned the farm or plantation where they were born. Mandy Jones of Lyman, Mississippi expressed, "My pappy's name was Wesley Young an' my mammy was Jinny Young . . . Atter de S'render lots o' de cullud folks change deir names, but some kept deir marster's names. My pappy's marster was named Stewart, but he changed his name back to Young, dat was de name of his ole marster in Maryland. His marster sole' him to a speculator when he was ten years ole . . ."[2]

Could I positively connect Pleasant Barr of Tippah County, Mississippi to Grandpa Bill? How did Pleasant Barr get to Mississippi? When? Where in South Carolina did he come from? I desperately wanted the answers to these questions. Not knowing the county in

43

South Carolina where they came from, I crashed into another brick wall. Could I knock this wall down as well? If so, how? I pondered.

After discovering Pleasant Barr, I called Cousin Ike and expressed ecstatically, "I found out Grandpa Bill's father's name! It was Pleas Barr!"

The name jarred his memory. He immediately shared, "Yeah, that's right! Boy, you are sure digging up some history! Grandpa Bill told us that his father was named Pleas, and that's where Uncle Pleas' name came from."

"So he talked about his father," I questioned.

"Oh yeah, all the time! He told us that his father was sold away, and they never saw him again. He used to talk about the day it happened. He said that they loaded his father on a wagon, and as the wagon was leaving the place, Grandpa just stood there and watched until the wagon was out of sight. It crossed some creek near the place where they were at, and it went down into a valley, and went off into the sunset. His father was gone but not forgotten. He talked about that so often because he always wondered where they took him. He was a young boy at the time."

I was floored by this vivid account but saddened by what it gave an account of.

"What about his mother? Did he talk about her, too," I asked with grave curiosity.

Bewildered, he stated, "You know, he didn't talk about his mother much. He talked about an older sister that took care of him, but I don't recall much of anything ever being said about his mother. I don't know what may have happened to her."

Apparently, Uncle Jimmy Reed also did not know much about Grandpa Bill's mother since the words "not known" were written on his death certificate.

Cousin Ike's account sent chills through me like water flowing down the mighty Mississippi River. He continued, "Grandpa sure did love his father though. I remember him telling us how he was such a fun-loving man who would always joke around with the other slaves there on the place. You know that was really hard on him to be separated from his father like that, never to see him again and never knowing where his father was at. He would always say that he watched his father being taken away, off into the sunset."

Awed by this new revelation, I commented, "I believe his father was taken to Ripley, Mississippi. There was a man named Pleasant Barr in the census records who lived near Ripley right after the Civil War. He was from South Carolina."

Cousin Ike responded stunningly, "That's not too far from here!"

"No more than about sixty-five miles from the Old Home Place." I added.

"Well, I am certain he was separated from his father in South Carolina, before they came here after the War, so he didn't know that his father was in Mississippi, too. He never talked about going to Ripley to visit him, so he must not have known that his father was there!" Cousin Ike was beyond astounded.

"I am going to verify if this Pleasant Barr in Ripley was truly his father," I promised.

As always, Cousin Ike closed the conversation, "Let me know what you dig up. Boy, you are on to something now!"

By this time, I had developed a nice rapport with a number of my older relatives that I did not hesitate to pick up the telephone to call them. I wanted to pique their brains about this new discovery.

Cousin Armentha recalled, "Grandpa Bill told us that his father's name was Pleas Barr. That's where my father's name came from. He said his father was sold away from them. I don't think he ever laid eyes on him again after he was sold."

Cousin Ike's baby brother, Rev. John Deberry Sr., recalled the following as well, "His father was sold away. He told us that. Ask my brother Ike about it. I am sure he told us that his father was sold."

Although Cousin John was thirteen years old when Grandpa Bill died, this fact remained fixated in his mind obviously because of the inhumanity of breaking up families. In her narrative, Delia Garlie of Montgomery, Alabama recalled the dreadfulness of separating families, ". . . Babies was snatched from dere mother's breas' an' sold to speculators. Chilluns was separated from sisters an' brothers an' never saw each other ag'in . . . Course dey cry; you think dey not cry when dey was sold lak cattle? I could tell you 'bout it all day, but even den you couldn't guess de awfulness of it."[3]

Angela soon provided me with a copy of her great-great-grandmother's pension file that she discovered at the National Archives in Washington, D.C. It was a goldmine. Amanda Young Barr tried unsuccessfully to get a widow's pension since her first husband had served in the Civil War. She first applied for a pension in 1872 and was rejected. Thirty-two years later, she reattempted and was rejected again. She tried unsuccessfully to conceal her cohabitation with Pleasant Barr as a legal marriage in order to get approved for a pension. If a woman remarried, pension payments were not given. She could, however, still receive the funds that had been due her before she remarried, even if she applied for the money after her remarriage.[4] The pension file contained sworn depositions that Amanda had to get from family members and neighbors to prove that she had been married to the soldier, Berry Young.

On July 31, 1916, special examiner Leighton Hope asked, "Now Aunt Amanda I want to know when you commenced to live with Pleas Barr?"

Amanda testified, "Well, I come back to Ripley, Mississippi, to Old Miss, and lived with her two months and they could not keep me and the children and Pleas Barr came along and I agreed to live with him and he agreed to help me raise my children. That was just about two months after surrender."

Mr. Hope questioned, "Then you commenced to living with him then?"

Amanda replied, "Yes. That was the first. We rented a house between us."

Hope further investigated, "Did you have any ceremony at that time?"

"We did not then and nor did we ever have any ceremony. I did live with him till he died. We did belong to the Church and went by the name Barr. I had only one child by him, Elijah Barr."[5]

On July 11, 1916, Wyatt Carter of Ripley gave the following testimony:

My age is fifty-two years old. I am farming. Ripley is my
P.O. address. I know Amanda and Pleas. I am not kin to her
and have no interest in this case. When I first recollect things
around here or so after the surrender I know that Amanda
and Pleas were living together and they continued to live
together as long as he lived. I do not know a thing about their
marriage. So far as I ever know they were lawfully married
but I did not know it and there never was anything said to the
contrary. They had one child named Lige Barr. Pleas Barr
died about ten years or more ago. He died here in Ripley.
Amanda was with him when he died. Aunt Amanda had
several children before she had Pleas Barr but I did not know
their father and do not know who he was. I do not know
what became of him. Aunt Amanda used to belong to the
Young Family here in Tippah County but I do not know
where Pleas Barr came from. He was here and living with
Mandy when I first knew him.[6]

On July 10, 1916, Amanda's daughter, Frances Nelson of Memphis, also known as Frank Nelson, testified:

She says that she did not marry Pleas Barr but she did live
with him from the time that I was very small till he died. She
had two children for him in Ripley. Lige Barr that lives here
in Memphis but I do not know what place. He did live on

47

Georgia Street, but I do not know what number. He is
married. He is about forty years of age. Mother lived with
Pleas Barr till he died in Ripley. Lige was grown when his
father died. I paid the funeral expenses in Ripley. Got a
coffin from Mr. Pfeiffer in Ripley. He was dead about eight
years when I came to Memphis and I have been in Memphis
eighteen years."[7]

Frances's testimony revealed that Pleasant Barr had died in Ripley in or
very near 1890. Grandpa Bill Reed had been in Mississippi for
approximately twenty-four years.

One deposition in the pension file contained the most significant
piece of information about Pleasant. Ripley resident Sam Edgerton's
oral account would prove to be invaluable. On July 12, 1916, he stated:

I knew Pleas Barr and Amanda Barr. I have known them
since before the war. **Pleas belonged to Giles about three or
four miles from Ripley**. I don't know why he took the name
of Barr after the War. Amanda belonged to Mr. Tandy Young
near Ripley, about five miles south of town. It was during the
War that I first knew of them living together. They were
together here in Ripley during the War and after the War a
while they had some sort of a ceremony. I did not see it but I
recollect the very night that she was said to be married to
Pleas Barr. They passed some sort of law that all people that
were living together without being married must marry
lawfully and they obeyed the law. I understood that that was
a law and I know they made them all marry here. After the
surrender Pleas changed his last name to Barr. I could not tell
you anything about the date that Pleas and Amanda married.
It was some three or four years after freedom. They lived
here together till Pleas died. He died here twenty years ago
or more. I did not know the first husband Amanda had. I

48

have heard that he was named Berry but I never knew him. She had only one child by Pleas. She had several by her first husband that I knew. About five that I knew. I knew Harriett, Frank, Violet, Henry, Alice, and another boy whose name I forgot. She had Lige, he was Pleas Barr's child.[8]

During the Civil War, Ripley, Mississippi was a hot-bed of war activity which proved to be advantageous to the lives of many enslaved African Americans in the county. Many were able to live a life of freedom during the Civil War due to the Union Army's heavy occupation of the area. Consequently, this spurned a mass exodus of escaped slaves to Tennessee, where they lived in contraband camps. Many of the men enlisted with the United States Colored Troops (USCT), including Amanda's first husband Berry Young, while Pleasant Barr, Amanda Young, and other enslaved families remained settled in Tippah County. Many of the enslaved were freed shortly after President Abraham Lincoln signed the Emancipation Proclamation on January 1, 1863, freeing all slaves in the southern Confederate states. Although most enslaved African Americans did not taste freedom until the end of the Civil War in 1865, many Tippah County Blacks were able to live out of bondage as early as January 1863. Amanda and her young children found refuge with Pleasant Barr after Berry Young left and did not return.

Discovering the surname of Pleasant Barr's last enslaver was like a demolition ball swinging towards my brick wall for its first strike. The 1860 U. S. Federal Census of Tippah County revealed that "Giles" was James Giles, the only Giles in the county. He was from South Carolina. James and Frances Giles appeared to have migrated to Mississippi sometime between 1857 and 1860, based on the ages and birthplaces reported for their two young sons; three-year-old John H. Giles was born in South Carolina, and one-month-old James Giles Jr. was born in Mississippi. The 1860 Tippah County Slave Schedule revealed that James Giles had four slaves. One of the males matched the profile of

Pleasant Barr – a forty-six-year-old black male. James Giles appeared to have possibly transported Pleasant Barr to Mississippi. How could I connect him to Grandpa Bill Reed? I wondered.

My move to Memphis, Tennessee in November 1996, to start a new position at an engineering firm, gave me immediate access to more records and to more family members. The genealogy and history department at the Memphis Public Library, which was just two miles from my employer, had census records for all of the southern states. During my lunch hour, I dashed to the library to locate James Giles in the 1850 U. S. Federal Census for South Carolina. Fortunately, he and his wife were found residing in Abbeville County. Within that one-hour break, I had uncovered a major breakthrough – a location in South Carolina to focus my research. My brick wall was beginning to crumble even more. However, since I was a young and rising civil engineer in a new major city, my research had to take a back seat. Days of mandatory overtime at work saturated my schedule. However, it did not claim the back seat for very long; the ancestors did not allow it.

On Friday evening, February 21, 1998, while working diligently to meet a deadline on a roadway design project, an e-mail from Michael Barr appeared in my inbox. He was touching base to see if I had progressed in my research. We had communicated on the Barr surname forum in America Online's genealogy section. He had done extensive research on the white Barr families in North and South Carolina. Michael had been unable to provide any clues to catapult my research because I had not determined where in South Carolina Grandpa Bill originated. I informed Michael that I recently determined the name of Grandpa Bill's father and that they may have hailed from Abbeville County. That was the only update that I had, and evidently, it was sufficient.

The next day, Michael responded with the following groundbreaking news:

Melvin, I have some good news for you! Pleasant is mentioned in Rev. William Barr's will. I will abstract the various Negroes mentioned in his will.

Rev. William Hampden Barr was born on August 6 or 8, 1778 in Rowan County, North Carolina. He married on August 18, 1812, to Rebecca Reid, who was born 1793 in S. C. She was the daughter of Hugh Reid. William died on January 9, 1843, in Abbeville County, South Carolina. He is buried at the Upper Long Cane Churchyard. He was the minister for many years. He and Rebecca had the following children: James, Samuel, Hugh Alexander, Elizabeth J., Margaret A., and William Hampden Barr, Jr.

Will abstract:

To my wife Rebecca my negroes, Glasgow and Rinda.

My daughter Margaret my negroes, Mariah, Sina, and Elbert.

My daughter Elizabeth my negroes, Frances, John, and Luther.

My son William my negroes, **Pleasant** and Sawney.

There is a line that says "the balance of my negroes I give and bequeath to my wife for and during her life or widowhood . ." Well Melvin, this is all I have. Hope it helps. Rebecca Barr died in 1863 and left a will. Only Glasgow and Rinda are mentioned. If you think of something else you want to ask, let me know.

Mike Barr[9]


"Oh my God!" I clamored at the computer screen, realizing that a major breakthrough had just unfolded.

I could not believe what I was reading. The Barr slave-holding family of Abbeville County, South Carolina was identified, and the wife and mother was a Reid. My brick wall was crumbling down even more. The demolition ball had made several strikes, and my wall was now becoming a pile of rubble. However, more was about to be uncovered.

Feeling genealogically rejuvenated, I spent the following day viewing the slave schedules at the Memphis Public Library instead of attending Sunday morning church service. The 1850 Abbeville County Slave Schedule reported Rebecca Barr with fourteen slaves. A number of the male slaves were under the age of ten; Grandpa Bill Reed was undoubtedly one of them. Rebecca's daughter, Margaret Barr, had six slaves, and her son, William Barr, owned two male slaves. They were all on one farm that was located two miles north of downtown Abbeville.

I continued scrolling through the slave schedule for the name Lem Reed. Cousin Ike had recalled that name from Grandpa Bill's stories. Within minutes, a jackpot was hit! A man named Lemuel Reid had owned ten slaves in 1850 in Abbeville County.

"This has to be Lem," I said confidently.

After several years of patience and perseverance, God had finally answered my prayers. At that moment, I felt that I had positively traced Grandpa Bill back to South Carolina. Through a preponderance of concrete evidence, I had found his long-lost father, and I had identified the names of his previous and last enslaver. I was overjoyed by this accomplishment. However, I was also saddened. Grandpa Bill never knew that his beloved father was just sixty-five miles away from him after slavery. They both lived the remainder of their lives in northern Mississippi. Much had been unearthed, but my journey of discovery was definitely not complete. There were too many unanswered questions.

On Saturday, March 14, 1998, I decided to visit the Memphis Public Library to research my maternal grandmother's family. The research of Grandpa Bill's roots had taken another temporary back seat. So I thought. I was informed by an Internet contact that I could find some valuable information about the white Milam Family in *The Heritage of Tate County, Mississippi*, published by the Tate County

Genealogical and Historical Society in 1991. The Milams were the slaveholding family of my maternal grandmother's paternal grandmother, Lucy Milam Davis.

I located the Tate County book on the shelf, but I immediately noticed *The Heritage of Tippah County, Mississippi* adjacent to it. I grabbed the Tippah County book first to quickly peek inside to see if, by chance, there may be something about Pleasant Barr. I was not hopeful since a number of the county history books I had viewed in the past contained little about the history of African Americans in the county. I turned to the index, and my heart rate rapidly increased with excitement. Pleasant Barr was listed. I immediately took the book to the table to see what was inside about my long-lost great-great-grandfather. Ironically, I left the Tate County book on the shelf. I turned to the page and read the following about the history of the St. Paul United Methodist Church:

> On February 21, 1870, the deed to the St. Paul Methodist
> Church was made and entered into agreement between W. R.
> Cole, the first party, and the trustees, the second party,
> Thomas Watts, **Pleasant Barr**, Anderson Pryor, who was the
> great-grandfather of Mr. Cowan White, at present the oldest
> male member of the congregation, and Abraham McCoy, the
> father of the late Dr. L. M. McCoy, President of Rust College.
> This board of trustees purchased this town lot described on
> the plan of the town of Ripley as 70 yards square in the
> southeast corner of block number 90, lying, and being in the
> State of Mississippi, and County of Tippah. This plot was
> purchased for the sum of one hundred dollars ($100.00);
> recorded March 1, 1870, in deed books "Y" pages 118-119.[10]

Working arduously to build America without compensation, many of the enslaved ancestors of African Americans suffered the emotional pain of being separated from their husbands, wives, sons, daughters, brothers, sisters, aunts, uncles, and cousins, never to see them again. Nevertheless, they continued on with their lives with an inner strength that was unspeakable – a strength that enabled them to survive an atrocious time in American history. Pleasant Barr was a survivor, and he went on with his life in Ripley, Mississippi after being taken away from Abbeville, South Carolina. This life entailed raising another family and serving as an active member of a local church in Ripley – one that he helped to build five years after slavery. I felt very proud to have his blood flowing through my veins.

I called Mom to share the church history with her since the father of Rust College's second African-American president, Dr. Lee Marcus McCoy, assisted Pleasant Barr and other trustee board members to secure a plot of land inside the town of Ripley in 1870 to construct St. Paul Church. She and Aunt Eartha were proud Rust College graduates. Mom was surprised to hear Dr. McCoy's name; she knew him very well. In fact, he was very instrumental in helping my grandmother to educate them at Rust. In 1956, a year after Granddaddy Simpson died, Mom and her sister had graduated from Geeter High School in Memphis, Tennessee, and they desired to attend college at Rust. They wanted to honor their parents' wishes of receiving a college education.

One Sunday morning, my grandmother loaded the family in the car and drove to Holly Springs to pay Dr. McCoy an unexpected visit. Someone had given her directions to his house on campus. Somehow, Grandma Minnie was able to talk to him, explaining that she was a recently widowed mother who needed financial assistance to send her daughters to Rust. Admiring my grandmother's tenacity, Dr. McCoy was very understanding and promised to see to it that they received financial aid to help defray the expenses. He kept his promise. Little did any of them know that his father and their long-lost great-grandfather, who was sold away from their Grandpa Bill in South Carolina, had built a church in Ripley, Mississippi five years after slavery. This exhibited an extraordinary meaning to the famous quote, "What a small world!"

The author of the church history was noted as Frederick Spight of Ripley. Angela Walton-Raji and I called him several days later on a three-way conference call after locating a contact number. We hoped that the church had records on Pleasant and Amanda that could provide us with more insight about their lives in Ripley after slavery. Our conversation was very delightful. He was quite elated to know that we were the descendants of one of the founders of his church.

Mr. Spight was a retired educator and a historian. He was quite knowledgeable about the history of his family, as well as African-American history in Tippah County. Interestingly, a man named Lewis Spight signed as a witness for Amanda on one of the affidavits in her pension file. Lewis was Mr. Spight's grandfather. Our histories were intertwined. Mr. Spight promised to check the surviving church records to see what else he could find on Pleasant and Amanda and their role at St. Paul.

The next day, I mailed Mr. Spight a letter of thank you, expressing my gratitude for talking with us on the telephone and his willingness to assist. A week later, I was delighted to receive a nice letter from him. He was, indeed, a man of his word. Mr. Spight typed the following:

Dear Mr. Collier,

It was indeed a pleasure to receive a letter from you this week since you and Angela have close ties here with St. Paul United Methodist Church. I feel that you are even closer to me – cousins or even closer. Even though I don't recall myself a writer as such, I am always doing research and at my age, I know more of the history surrounding us than most people here. Therefore, I'm always called on by both Black and white for articles for publication for the newspaper or other historical publications. Just last week, the local paper devoted several sections of the paper to the growth and development of the school system of Tippah County. I was one of the first to be interviewed for the project since I was in the founding of the first black high school of Ripley.

It is so interesting that you have been tracing your family roots for almost four years. I knew that Pleasant Barr was one of the founding fathers of St. Paul Church, but I was not able to find too much on him before most of the church records were destroyed. This is all I could find:

In 1870, when the church was founded, Mr. Barr, who came from South Carolina, was fifty-six years old. He was married to Amanda, who was thirty-eight and came from Tennessee. They had six children and two grandchildren. The children were Harriett, 17, Frank, 13, Violet, 11, Alice, 7, Elijah, 3. The grandchildren were Alma and Rosa.

Since you have found more on him than I have, I would like to have your version or you make the necessary corrections in what I have.

It was certainly a pleasure to talk with you on the telephone and to receive a letter from you. Let's keep this communication going. I will be glad to have you visit me in the near future on the weekend and go to church with me on Sunday. Even though we are a small church, we have worship service every Sunday.

For the past two months, I have been ill. In fact, I stayed in the hospital for two weeks. I am now on dialysis three days a week, but I am doing remarkably well. I still do just about all of my daily activities except drive the car, but I'll start driving again next week.

Sincerely yours, Frederick L. Spight[11]

Cousin Leroy Frazier and I decided to pay homage to Pleasant Barr by visiting St. Paul Church. Sadly, shortly after our correspondence, Frederick Spight's health took a turn for the worst. God called him into His kingdom on August 2, 1999, a little over a year after our initial contact. Upon arriving at St. Paul, we were warmly greeted by his niece. Other members of the church were also thrilled about our visit. The weird-sounding name, "Pleasant Barr," was a permanent fixture in their church history. How thrilling it was to tell the congregation that we were his direct descendants who had found his whereabouts. The expressions on their faces as I relayed our family history were of wonderment and fascination. How many times does a visiting stranger reveal to a church congregation that one of its founders was a man who was sold away from his first family during slavery, never to see them again, and that we were the descendants of that first family who had traced him back to this church.

The present-day church was erected in 1980. According to Mr. Spight, the first church structure was a one-room building approximately thirty by forty feet facing the east. The provisions of the deed stated that the church was to be used for a place of divine worship and a school to educate the community's children. After not receiving an education due to the unjustly laws of slavery, many former slaves, like the St. Paul Board of Trustees, were proactive in educating their children during Reconstruction, despite the great obstacles of racial injustice and very few economic resources. They risked their lives to educate the people of the community, children and adults, as educated African Americans were considered a threat to the status quo of the racist South.

Despite the dangers, Pleasant Barr and the board pooled their meager resources together to build a multi-facet building that was to be a church and a school, which was very common throughout the South. The first building was replaced by another frame structure on the southeast corner of the lot in the latter 1800s. In 1949, this second building was eventually turned, enlarged, and bricked. According to

The first structure of St. Paul Methodist Church in Ripley, Mississippi. Pleasant Barr and other board of trustee members secured a plot of land in the town of Ripley in 1870 to construct this church. Source: St. Paul Methodist Church

The second structure of St. Paul Methodist Church in Ripley, Mississippi. In 1949, the first structure was turned, enlarged, and bricked.

Gone but not forgotten.

*The current structure of St. Paul Methodist Church in Ripley, Mississippi, which was built in 1980.*

Mr. Spight, St. Paul was a model church of its size in the Upper Mississippi Conference, and they hosted the Annual Conference the following year. With the help of the Volunteers in Mission, a new brick parsonage was built on the site of the original church in 1980.[12]

After church service, one of the church deacons, Mr. James Johnson, offered to take us to the home of the church's oldest-living member, Mrs. Myrtle Gray, who was not in attendance that Sunday. We happily agreed. Our ancestor had died long before Mrs. Gray was born. Nevertheless, she was very familiar with his name, and she greeted us with a gigantic smile when we told her who we were.

As we were conversing with Mrs. Gray in her living room, we noticed on the television that bad weather was going to strike the Ripley area within an hour. Our day had been filled with lots of sunshine and pleasant temperatures. Several severe thunderstorm warnings were being issued for several counties to the west, and the approaching storm system was headed east towards Ripley.

We decided to shorten our visit with Mrs. Gray and get on the highway back to Memphis before the bad weather arrived. As we were leaving her house, Deacon Johnson noticed the next-door neighbor, Mrs. Elizabeth Rogers, sitting on her porch. He asked, "Would you all like to go over there to visit with Mrs. Rogers? She too is an elder member of this community."

As I opened my mouth to decline his offer, I suddenly said, "Okay, but for a few minutes. It's going to storm soon." We proceeded over to Mrs. Rogers's house.

Mrs. Rogers possessed such fair skin that she could have easily been mistaken for a white woman from a distance. After Deacon Johnson's introduction, she said loudly with a deep, Southern drawl, "Y'all come up here and have a seat."

I responded, "We just wanted to say to hello. We won't bother you. It looks like a storm is headed this way."

"Baby, y'all ain't botherin' me. I like to get visitors, 'specially from two handsome young men."

She had never laid eyes on Cousin Leroy and me, or even knew where we had come from, but her friendliness and her welcoming spirit were quite comforting. We took a seat.

I shared unenthusiastically, "We are just here in Ripley to pay our respects to one of our ancestors who was brought here during slavery." Since Pleasant Barr had been dead for over one hundred years, I did not expect to learn anything from this quick visit.

Mrs. Rogers asked, "Who your people?"

"My great-great-grandfather was named Pleasant Barr. He was sold away and brought to Ripley around 1859. His family never saw him again, but I located him here and learned how he helped to start St. Paul Church."

Mrs. Rogers quickly exclaimed, "I heard that name before. My grandfather used to talk about him!"

"What!" I asked shockingly, "Who was your grandfather?"

"Papa's name was Sam Edgerton," she said proudly.

Gone but not forgotten.

*Mrs. Elizabeth Rogers and Melvin J. Collier in Ripley, Mississippi*

"What! Oh my God! You got to be kidding me! This is unbelievable!" I shouted.

Tears immediately flowed down my face as I sat there in complete awe for two minutes. After pulling myself together, I eagerly explained, "Oh, my God! Your grandfather was the very person who provided crucial information to the government in 1916 that helped me to trace my great-great-grandfather's history. If it was not for his testimony, we would not have known as much as we know now."

"You don't say! Well, I am so happy to hear that, baby! Papa talked about him often. I remember because the name Pleasant Barr sounded so strange to me. He and Papa were good friends."

Indeed, Mrs. Rogers was accurate. Sam Edgerton had testified that he had known Pleasant Barr since before the Civil War started in 1861.

Mrs. Rogers was thrilled, but probably not as thrilled as I was. Before leaving her home, I got a chance to thank Sam Edgerton by giving his granddaughter a big hug. This visit with Mrs. Rogers confirmed for us that Pleasant Barr had been guiding this trip to Ripley all along. He was definitely not going to let us leave there without talking to Mrs. Rogers.

Upon leaving Mrs. Rogers' house, the clouds had turned ominous as the severe thunderstorm approached the sleepy town. Since we had not eaten since that morning, Cousin Leroy and I decided to wait out the storm there in Ripley and eat a meal at Kentucky Fried Chicken. As we sat and ate our dinner, the dark clouds opened, the rain poured, the wind howled, and lightning struck repeatedly upon the small town.

Very quietly, we sat in Kentucky Fried and reflected on the amazing day we just had. We felt Pleasant Barr's presence; the pouring raindrops were his tears. He cried about the day he was placed on a wagon and taken away from the Barr farm near Abbeville, South Carolina, while his young son Bill stood there and starred as the wagon rode off into the sunset. He cried about never seeing his family ever again. He cried about the struggles he and millions of other slaves in the South endured for over two hundred years – struggles that we cannot even image today. He cried tears of joy because we came to Ripley. He was gone but not forgotten.

Downtown Ripley, Mississippi (west side of square) in 1890, around the year when Pleasant Barr died there at the age of about 76. Source: Tippah Treasures, Tippah County Development Foundation, Courtesy of Ripley Public Library

# *Chapter 4*

## **Reid not Reed**

ousin Carolyn Knox questioned, "When did we go from Reid with an 'i' to Reed with two e's?"

"I really don't know. Quite possibly, Grandpa Bill or perhaps one of his older children just arbitrarily began to spell it that way," I answered. I had already posed that question several years earlier, but I had little hope of ever finding any documentation to answer that question.

With much curiosity about her great-great-grandfather, she theorized, "Grandpa Bill probably wanted to have a different spelling of his name to reflect his freedom. He was a free man, and a different spelling would have symbolized it."

"That's very possible," I replied. Cousin Carolyn obviously wanted to believe her theory. I loved her historical analysis. But, it was an unproven theory.

There were a number of possibilities for the alternate spelling. In the 1870 census, Grandpa Bill's surname was spelled "Reed." He was not found in the 1880 census. However, in 1900, the census-taker ironically wrote "Read." In the later censuses, the name was recorded as "Reed."

Grandpa Bill did not receive an education due to the unjustly laws of the land that denied enslaved African Americans from even learning the alphabets. One of the goals of American slavery was to prevent any advancement of the African-American mind. To do otherwise would have contradicted the preposterous ideologies of western society that deemed African Americans as sub-human. Plausibly, someone, perhaps the 1870 census-taker, could have loudly spelled his surname with two e's, and Grandpa Bill may have continued on with that particular spelling when asked his name. Despite the spelling and our theories, his surname came from the last slave-owner, Lemuel Reid. I knew that researching and learning the history of the white Reids would ultimately lead to facts about his history.

"Contacting the Slave-owner's Descendants" is a subject that is often discussed among many African-American researchers on AfriGeneas.com and other Internet forums. In order to trace back beyond 1865, the slave-owner's family has to be researched just as much as your own family, if not more. Many times, the descendants of the slave-owning families possess valuable information.

In contacting them, some of the experiences of African-American researchers have been fruitful. However, some experiences have not. With some, initial communications with the white descendants that only discussed names, places, and dates started off well. The e-mails continued until their identity and historical connection were revealed. In some cases, the historical connections are biological ones. Then, the e-mail responses from the white descendants would come to a screeching halt. Some were either uncomfortable discussing the slaves their ancestors owned or they were unwilling to acknowledge that a liaison had occurred between their esteemed ancestor and an enslaved girl or woman and the child or children that resulted. Some were in denial that their ancestors even owned slaves. This was not my experience with the Reids.

Fortunately, I discovered that the Reids of Abbeville County, South Carolina had been researched quite extensively. Many of the white Reid descendants had posted on several online genealogy forum boards and mailing lists and were willing to communicate. I chose not to conceal my historical connection, and the communication has been conducive. I was soon led to Lemuel Reid's great-grandson, Wayne Reid of Florida. He possessed Lemuel's diaries and had transcribed his 1860 diary. He later transcribed his 1861 diary. I was given his mailing address and urged to contact him. Leaving no stone unturned, I did not waste any time drafting a letter to him explaining my historical connection to Lemuel Reid and expressing my desire for more information about the Reid Family, specifically any documentation concerning the family slaves. I mailed the letter and whispered a prayer for great results.

Several days later, my phone rang and the caller I.D. displayed "Wayne Reid." Nervously, I picked up the telephone after several rings. This was the first time I had communicated via phone with a descendant of my ancestor's enslaver. How will the conversation proceed? What will he say? What will I say? Will the events of slavery be discussed? Certainly, it will have to be the primary topic since I was in search of my enslaved ancestors. On the fourth ring, I answered the telephone to travel down this new road of discovery.

Wayne Reid, a South Carolina native, was an elderly man who shared a passion for genealogy. He understood the struggles of genealogy, especially for African-American researchers who wanted to document their enslaved ancestors. He was flabbergasted that I was only in my twenties. To my sheer delight, he shared with me how the 1860 diary and a cotton-picker list that Lemuel Reid compiled in 1861 may be of some assistance since a number of slaves were mentioned, including one named Bill. Coincidentally, he had a brother named Bill Reid, who was a Clemson University professor and an avid genealogist. Wayne had transcribed the 1860 diary in 1994, and he kindly offered to send me a book.

Before ending our conversation, he shared that in the early 1950s, he met an elderly man in Abbeville who claimed that his father had been a slave of Lemuel Reid. The man shared that his father referred to the pre-Civil War days as the "good times." Wayne and I both believed that this was certainly not a shared sentiment among most formerly enslaved African Americans. However, the comment indicated that Lemuel may have treated his slaves better than most slave-owners.

As promised, a package from Wayne arrived several days later, on Saturday, May 9, 1998. Enclosed was *The 1860 Diary of Lemuel Reid, an Abbeville District, South Carolina Planter*. The diary was a rarity and a goldmine. Enclosed in the package was a rather interesting and comical typewritten letter. Wayne typed the following:

Dear Melvin,

Thanks again for your delightful letter. I called my brother in Clemson and sister-in-law in Abbeville and read it to them. Their reaction was the same as mine; both asked me to send them a copy. Bill said that he had no information on Lemuel's slaves that I did not already have, so the best source is probably the list I am also sending which was copied from the inside cover of Lemuel's 1861 diary. It was copied by Reid Dusenberry of N.C. and I have not yet transcribed it.

I was curious why Lemuel kept a record of how much cotton each person picked until I read an entry in his diary which said "paid negroes what I owed them." I was never aware that they were paid anything, but in any case, it probably wasn't much.

I have been somewhat amused by the Reid family's reaction to the book. The men, including me, think Lemuel was something of a crab, but the women despise him. In over two years of diaries he only referred to his wife by name once, otherwise only as "wife." One of my female cousins was overjoyed when she visited the cemetery and saw that Sophia outlived him by many years. And I was visualizing Sophia as Scarlett O'Hara until someone sent me her picture. With all due respect to the dead, I think she is probably as ugly a woman as I've ever seen.

Again, I was extremely pleased to hear from you and only regret that I can not offer you more help. Please keep me informed of your progress. I do not have E-mail as "wife" will not let a computer in the house. My fax is (XXX) XXX-XXXX. I wish you the best.

Sincerely,
Wayne[1]

The Reid Family's presence in Abbeville District, South Carolina began with Lemuel's great-grandfather, George Reid. Born in Ulster, Ireland on December 23, 1719, George, his wife Margaret, their infant daughter Rose, and his brothers migrated to America in 1745. They first settled in Lancaster County, Pennsylvania and lived on Swatawra Creek for a short while. They were among many Scotch-Irish immigrants who came to America in the eighteenth century, crossed the mountains to the Pennsylvania frontiers, and later settled down the valleys into Virginia and the Carolinas. Famine struck Ireland during the 1740s and over 400,000 perished. Consequently, this caused a tremendous exodus of primarily Ulstermen to America.[2] Around 1750, George and his family, which now included two additional children, Samuel and Ann, traveled into the Shenandoah Valley of Virginia and settled for a short time in Augusta County, Virginia, where two additional children, Margaret and Joseph, were born.

*Lemuel Reid*
*(October 26, 1818 – May 17, 1867)*

*Sophia Weston White Reid*
*(January 18, 1824 – November 23, 1896)*

*Source: "The 1860 Diary of Lemuel Reid, an Abbeville District, South Carolina Planter" by Wayne A. Reid*

In April 1763, George received a Royal Land Grant for land along Long Cane Creek in Abbeville District, South Carolina. From 1729 to the beginning of the Revolutionary War in 1776, the Crown of England was responsible for the issuance of royal land grants for land in North and South Carolina, supervised by the Royal Governor of the Colony. Every adult who paid his way to the Carolinas was entitled to fifty acres of land, and he or she was also entitled to fifty acres for every adult whose ship fare or passage was paid by them. They were also given land for each child they transported into the Carolinas. The first settlers had to not only struggle against the physical elements of the environment, but they also faced danger from the Cherokee Indians, who naturally considered them unwelcomed guests on their ancestral land.

After a 1755 treaty with the Cherokee Indians, who ceded a great portion of upper South Carolina to the colonists, the area experienced an influx of Scotch-Irish families from Virginia and Pennsylvania. Before 1755, the area had been vastly uninhabited by whites with the exception of a few traders and hunters. By the time of the Revolutionary War, the upcountry boasted a population of nearly 80,000, with the Scotch-Irish Presbyterians being the largest group of Europeans.[3] Upon settling in Abbeville District in 1763, George built and operated a grist mill. He was a member of the Long Cane Society and was one of the founders of the Upper Long Cane Presbyterian Church.

Like many of the Scotch-Irish immigrants, George Reid acquired African slave labor which increased the prosperity of planters. Perhaps, he acquired slaves after settling into a colony that boasted a majority Black population. By the end of the 1760-1770 decade, a majority African population had prevailed in South Carolina for several decades. Africans had outnumbered whites in the colony at a ratio of at least two to one.[4] Furthermore, nearly 19,000 Africans were transported into Charleston, South Carolina during the 1760s alone, and from 1771 to 1775, in just a five-year period, over 19,000 more

Africans were transported into the province. Historian Gwendolyn Midlo Hall asserts that over half of all Atlantic slave voyages into South Carolina arrived between 1751 and 1775.[5] Over 40 percent of the captured Africans transported to the British colonies before the American Revolution passed through Charleston, South Carolina, making it the largest port during the transatlantic slave trade. Throughout most of the eighteenth century, the colony had a higher density of Blacks and a lower percentage of whites than any other part of the North American mainland.[6]

A majority of the African population in South Carolina was concentrated on low-country plantations. By 1790, eleven of eighteen low-country rural parishes were more than 80 percent Black.[7] Many low-country slaves were sold upriver to planters in the upcountry. When George Reid wrote his will in 1786, he bequeathed to his children twelve slaves – Bet, Mille, Senna, Adam, Munmuth, Phillis, Tom, Prue, Primiss, Boson, Isaac, and Hannah. Plausibly, some of them may have been within three generations from Africa. Some may have also been directly from Africa. George died around 1790; the exact year is unknown.

On May 8, 1776, George's daughter, Margaret, married Hugh Reid, quite possibly his nephew.[8] Marriages between first cousins were common among the Scotch-Irish. Known to his colleagues as "Squire" Reid, Hugh became a vast land-owner in Abbeville District and was an elder at Upper Long Cane Church for over forty-five years. He died in 1829 at the old age of 83. In his will, he bequeathed to his children over 900 acres of land in Abbeville District, 140 acres in Union County, Indiana, and seven slaves. His will indicated that he had distributed to his children a large portion of his estate before his death. His wife Margaret had died on December 27, 1818.

Hugh and Margaret Reid had the following nine children:

1. *Rev. George Reid*, born 1777, died 1836

2. *Margery Reid*, born 1778, and died Oct. 1856 in Pontotoc County, Mississippi. She married Ebenezer Miller in 1800 and they later moved to Pontotoc County, Mississippi where he died in 1848.

3. *Jane Reid*, born about 1780.

4. *Margaret Reid*, born 1782 and died before 1835, Jefferson County, Mississippi. She married Joseph Miller in 1800 in Abbeville District. He died in 1829, Jefferson County, Mississippi.

5. *James Reid*, born 1784 and died in 1868. He moved to Union County, Indiana before 1813 and then on to Lee County, Iowa, where he died.

6. *Elizabeth Reid*, born 1786 and died in 1838 in Abbeville District. She married Robert C. Wilson in 1810. He died in 1832 in Abbeville District.

7. *Samuel Reid*, born 1788 and died in 1857 in Abbeville District. He married Elizabeth Ann Wilson who died in 1872. Samuel & Elizabeth were the parents of **Lemuel Reid**.

8. *Rosie Reid*, born about 1790.

9. *Rebecca Reid*, born 1793 and died in 1863 in Abbeville District. She married *Rev. William H. Barr* in 1812. He died in 1843 in Abbeville District.

Hugh and Margaret's youngest son, Samuel Reid, received the bulk of his father's land as well as his home. The house is extant and is located four miles north of Abbeville on the Level Land Highway. Samuel married Elizabeth Ann Wilson on June 20, 1815, and they had six children: Mary Reid Wilson (1816-1872), wife of John R. Wilson; Jane Reid (1817-1818); Lemuel Reid (1818-1867); James Caldwell Reid (1820-1864); Margaret Elizabeth Reid (1822-??); and Alexander Mack Reid (1830-1855). Samuel died on July 24, 1857; he left his land to his wife Elizabeth and daughter, Mary Wilson.

Lemuel Reid amassed as much as 653 acres of land near his father's plantation. According to Wayne Reid, his plantation was known to the local populace as the "Reid Place." In Cousin Ike Deberry's memories of Grandpa Bill's stories, he had often referred to it as the "place." On August 27, 1860, the Reid Place was the home of Lemuel, his wife Sophia White (1824-1896), and their eight children, John W., 19, James A., 15, Harvey W., 13, Samuel O., 11, Mary V., 8, Alexander Mack, 5, Fanny W., 3, and Thomas H., six months, as reported by the census-taker. Five additional children were born after 1860. The census-taker also reported that two teenagers, Samuel Martin, 15, and James Martin, 13, also lived on the plantation.

The 1850 Abbeville County Slave Schedule reported Lemuel with ten slaves. By 1860, his slaveholdings increased to twenty slaves, giving him a personal estate value of $23,390, equivalent to a 2008-value of over a half a million dollars. These enslaved African Americans lived in five slave houses, located in the area known as the slave quarters, constituting a small plantation – one that contained four horses, four mules, eight milk cows, two oxen, twelve cattle, twenty-nine sheep, and fifty hogs, according to the 1860 agricultural census. In contrast, most of the 400,000 slave-owners in the South in the 1850s owned ten or fewer slaves.[9] Additionally, Lemuel possessed a relatively young work force. In 1860, the oldest slave on the Reid Place was a thirty-six-year-old male and the youngest slaves were a six-month-old male and a six-month-old female.

Interestingly, Lemuel's 1860 diary contained daily entries that were brief yet very insightful. The entries provided a snapshot of social, farm, and slave activity on the eve of the Civil War in Abbeville County. Lacking appropriate punctuation, each entry was one very long sentence that consisted of several phrases running together. Each phrase represented a different happening of the day. He started each entry with a two, three, or four-word synopsis of the weather with brief descriptions like "morning clear and pleasant" or "still cloudy." Only the entry for April 8th was missing. One can deduce that Lemuel had a clear knack for detail and order. He kept other diaries for the years 1861, 1862, and 1863 that are in the family's possession. Currently, no diaries pre-dating 1860 have been found, although the family believes that he kept them for earlier years.

Referring to slaves as "hands," Lemuel recorded the following names in his 1860 diary: Brown, Kate, Dropshot, Louisa, Isaac, Abram, Israel, Pleas/Pleasant, Bob, Nathan/Nat, Bill/Billy, Jobe, Old Ben, Ned, Nance, Glasgo, Aron, Lewis, and Sam. Some of them were not owned by him but had been hired out to him by their enslavers. The names Pleas and Pleasant immediately caught my eye. Was he Grandpa Bill's brother or cousin? I wondered. Many young boys were commonly named after their fathers. Enslaved boys were more prone to be named after their fathers since fathers were often forcibly separated from their children than mothers.[10] Perhaps, Glasgo was Rev. Glasgow Wilson, who migrated to Mississippi with Grandpa Bill and had married him and Momma Sarah Partee in 1871. Cousin Ike Deberry claimed that he was a close relative, perhaps an older brother, an older cousin, or an uncle. Interestingly, Lemuel's brother-in-law and sister, John R. and Mary Reid Wilson, lived adjacent to him and may have been the last enslavers of Glasgow.

Lemuel Reid mentioned "Bill" or "Billy" in seven of his diary entries. Wayne Reid noted that Bill/Billy was a slave, and I had no reason to believe that he was not Grandpa Bill Reed. He wrote the following (for clarity, semi-colons were added to separate the phrases):

Wednesday Feb. 8th – Cloudy and drizzly; sent **Bob** to mill with stock; hands building fences at brick yard; sowed on sewing machine till dinner; J. H. Means called; Fanny sick; walked out to where hands were working; ground very well; Mr. Gilmore and wife called and sat awhile; Mrs. Baskin gone home; **Billy** took her in carriage

Friday Feb. 17th – Cool and hazy, cleared away beautiful; suffered last night with pain in my side, feel bad; Junius Martin sick with cold; Margaret spending the day with us; walked out to field; **Billy** laid up with cold; Edwin gone home; clouded up in evening; commenced raining at dark

Thursday, Feb. 23rd – Clear and warm; all hands hauling out manure; commenced trimming peach trees; sent **Bill** to depot for groceries; James Means called and told us of cousin N. J. Bowie and Roberts arrival; Stark Martin sick with cold; quite warm tonight

Thursday, March 22nd – Cold with white frost; **Israel**, **Nathan**, and **Brown** making rails where fence was burned; **Aron** and **Dropshot** hauling manure in orchard; **Billy** and **Kate** broke potatoe patch; **Bob** laying off orchard; went to town; took dinner at J. H. Wilson; Henry Sharp got flour from me

Saturday, May 5th – Beautiful day; A. E. Leslie called; walked with him over farm, see corn knee high, wheat and oats looking better; finished hoeing corn; hands working in their patches; sent **Bill** to depot again, but no better success; John at home from Erskine

Thursday, August 2nd – Clear & warm; killed mutton, took it to town; brought Rev. E. R. Singletary to our house; sent the corn to mill; spent evening entertaining Singletary; no appearance of rain; all hands plowing cotton; **Billy** came home after night from mill

Friday, October 26th – Very warm; sent Bud & **Bill** to take carriage & buggy to take friends to J. R. Wilson's; A. E. Leslie called; all hands picking cotton; thrashed out peas, had 10

*"The Reid Place," just north of Abbeville, South Carolina, as it stood in 2009 in its dilapidated state. It was built in 1861 while Grandpa Bill Reed was a slave on this farm. The house was abandoned in 1995. In 2010, the house was moved to a new location in Abbeville County by its new owner, Bill Rogers, and is currently being renovated. It's ironic that the new owner is named Bill.*

bushels; Harvey Wilson to dinner; rode to town in evening;
John complaining; Bud & Bill stayed till night; L. C. Wilson
hauling cotton to gin *(Wayne Reid noted that Bud was Lemuel's
son, Samuel Orren Reid.)*

Social life on the Reid Place was quite active in 1860. Lemuel had
an amazing number of dinner guests and overnight guests throughout
the entire year. According to Wayne Reid, his dinner table was
actually three large walnut tables combined; it was still in use as late as
the early 1900s. When the end tables were used to extend the large
center table, fourteen adults could be comfortably seated. The table
possessed cord webbing underneath where the family silver was
periodically stored during the Civil War to hide it from wandering
Yankee soldiers. During the Great Depression, the table was sold to a
woman from New York City for one hundred dollars.[11] The owner,
Lemuel's daughter-in-law, Annie White Reid, had experienced tough
economic times like many during this financial downturn in American
history.

Two of Lemuel's many friends and family members who ate and
socialize often at that dinner table were Rebecca Barr, who he called
"Aunt Barr," and her son, William Jr. Perhaps, at this dinner table, the
Barrs decided that they would sell Grandpa Bill and probably others,
including his younger sister Mary, to him. Maybe Rebecca decided to
make this monetary transaction at this table to help finance her
youngest son's move to Mississippi, not caring that this sell would
separate a young boy from his family. A tip from several online Reid
researchers revealed that William Barr Jr. established residency in
Pontotoc County, Mississippi shortly before 1860, but he traveled back
to South Carolina several times in 1860.

Because of Lemuel's close relationship with his paternal aunt and
her children, Grandpa Bill still saw the Barrs often after he was sold to
Lemuel. On Tuesday, January 10, Rebecca Barr, his mother Elizabeth
Reid, and his brother-in-law, J. R. Wilson, were all overnight guests on

the Reid Place. Nearly a month later, he made the following notation on Monday, February 6th that stated, "Surprised in the evening by the arrival of William Barr from Mississippi with Margaret's negroes." Wayne Reid noted that Margaret was William's sister, Margaret Barr. In 1843, she had inherited three slaves named Mariah, Sina, and Elbert per the instructions of her father's will. Apparently, William Jr. had taken them to Mississippi, possibly Pontotoc County, and brought them back to South Carolina. He spent the night on the Reid Place after his arrival. On Tuesday, February 7th, Lemuel noted, "Wm. Barr stayed until after dinner." Two days later, Thursday, February 9th, William and Rebecca were again overnight guests. Then, on Saturday, February 11th, he wrote, "Wm. Barr took dinner with us and started for Mississippi." Barr had stayed a total of five days in Abbeville, a much shorter time than the time it would take for him to return to Pontotoc County, Mississippi. He visited Abbeville later in the year and was in Abbeville during the Christmas holiday. On Wednesday, October 31st, Lemuel wrote the following entry:

> Cloudy & warm; sent corn to mill; did not get it and had to go
> back; wrote letter to James C. Reid (his brother); Wm. Barr
> took them to town and mailed; Mother came down to spend a
> few days with us; J. J. Leslie staying all night.

On Wednesday, December 26th, Lemuel Reid wrote:

> Clear & beautiful; went out with Ben to hunt squirrels, killed
> one; Ben and family gone to visit his wifes father; Aunt Barr &
> William spending the day with us; A. E. Leslie called, also Ben
> Means; pleasant day.

On a typical plantation, many field hands rose before dawn, prepared their meals, fed the livestock, and then proceeded to the fields before sunrise. If there was a failure to be in the fields by a specified time, this often resulted in several lashes from the overseer.[12] Lemuel did not write about the presence of an overseer, and the 1860 U. S. Federal Census gives no indication that a resident overseer lived on the Reid Place. Nevertheless, the work that was performed on the Reid Place seemed infinite. On nearly all farms and plantations, a rest season did not exist; the climate was always considered adequate for labor. Therefore, the slaves were economically active the entire year. After working from "can't to can't," the exhausted slaves on many plantations typically had to care for their livestock, put away tools, and cook their meals before the horn sounded bedtime in the quarters.[13] Lemuel never mentioned in his diary that he or anyone ranged any bells to alert the enslaved laborers. On the other hand, over fifty tasks were performed by the slaves throughout the year. These laborious tasks included the following:

1. cutting wood
2. railing lumber
3. making rails
4. hauling wood
5. splitting cord wood
6. framing smokehouse and carriage house
7. getting timber for carriage house
8. repairing fence
9. cutting briars in stubble field
10. putting up coal kiln in bottom
11. dressing plank for smoke house
12. building fences
13. plowing
14. weather boarding smoke house
15. rolling logs
16. hauling posts for garden
17. hewing posts for garden fence
18. hauling stock to mill

19. clearing land
20. chopping in clearing
21. fanning wheat and sending to mill
22. husking and shelling corn
23. breaking up land
24. hauling manure
25. planting cotton
26. breaking ground for potatoes
27. hoeing cotton
28. bedding cotton land
29. scattering manure
30. ginning and packing cotton
31. cutting ditches on branch
32. planting corn
33. knocking down corn stocks
34. succoring corn
35. plowing and hoeing corn
36. laying off orchard
37. cutting barley
38. breaking potato patch
39. preparing and planting potatoes
40. plowing up potatoes
41. filling under drains and clearing up swamp
42. clipping sheep
43. hauling sheep
44. making gates
45. planting negro patch
46. running water furrow between cotton beds
47. cutting wheat
48. sunning wheat
49. cutting oats
50. suckering corn and planting slips
51. pulling fodder

52. hauling load of fodder
53. tying up fodder in willow bottoms
54. working garden
55. pealing willows
56. making baskets
57. sowing barley and turnip patch
58. killing hogs
59. salting meat

During most of January 1860, the slaves on the Reid Place were mostly engaged in cutting and hauling wood, making rails, and building a fence, a smokehouse, and a carriage house. On Wednesday, January 18, some of the slaves started plowing the land in preparation for planting cotton, while others continued building a fence and performing a multitude of other tasks. Plowing continued until Monday, February 20, as Lemuel noted on that day, "Hands finished up breaking up (the land) and commenced hauling manure." Livestock manure was and continues to be a good fertilizer for the soil, providing such nutrients as nitrogen, phosphorus, and potassium. Manure was scattered on the freshly plowed land before cotton seeds were planted. Bedding of the cotton land continued until Saturday, March 10.

The following Monday, March 12, the slaves were given an opportunity to fertilize their own gardens, commonly known as "Negro patches," in which they raised their own fruits and vegetables. Lemuel's diary entries indicated that Saturdays were usually the days when the slaves worked their own patches. However, since they had been busy bedding the cotton fields on this particular Saturday, they were allowed to tend to their own gardens the following Monday. The next day, Tuesday, March 13, the slaves started breaking up the bottom land – the description for low-lying areas near a river, lake, or creek which often flooded. Plowing on the bottom land continued for the rest of the week, and on Monday, March 19, corn was finally planted.

Lemuel noted, "Commenced planting corn, ground in fine order; running six plows; think I can plant most of my corn in 3 days." They finished two days later.

Cotton-planting on the Reid Place began on Monday, April 9th, and cotton-picking began just shy of five months later, on Thursday, August 30th. Cousin Ike had shared how Grandpa Bill communicated to his family that he was the water boy who carried buckets of water to the other slaves working in the field. This task was likely performed during his early enslavement on the Barr farm, since children between the ages of six and ten were typically active as water carriers. Also, Grandpa Bill relayed that Lemuel considered him a good plow boy, to justify his human acquisition from his Barr relatives. Very likely, he spent many days in the field, especially between April and September, plowing the fields with the other slaves. There were numerous entries in Lemuel's diary during this time frame which indicated that on some days, all of the slaves on the Reid Place were in the fields chopping, bedding, planting, plowing, or hoeing. Observing slaves in the field on a much larger plantation near Natchez, Mississippi, Frederick Olmstead provided the following description of this extensive labor:

> We found in the field thirty ploughs, moving together,
> turning the earth from the cotton plants, and from thirty to
> forty hoers, the latter mainly women, with a black driver
> walking about among them with a whip, which he often
> cracked at them, sometimes allowing the lash to fall lightly
> upon their shoulders. He was constantly urging them also
> with his voice. All worked very steadily, and though the
> presence of a stranger on the plantation must have been a
> most unusual occurrence, I saw none raise or turn their heads
> to look at me. Each gang was attended by a "water-toter," that
> of the hoe-gang being a straight, sprightly, plump little black
> girl, whose picture, as she stood balancing the bucket upon
> her head, shading her bright eyes with one hand, and holding

out a calabash with the other to maintain her poise, would have been a worthy study for Murillo.[14]

Grandpa Bill was listed on several cotton-picker lists that were found in Lemuel Reid's 1861 diary. He had kept a record of how much cotton each of the slaves picked. On one list, Grandpa Bill was the third highest cotton-picker, having picked ninety-eight pounds of cotton in one day. Israel had picked 137 pounds, while Bob came in second at 119 pounds. Even more surprising, on Monday, February 4th, Lemuel noted the following in his diary, "Called up all my negroes & paid them off what I owed them." Plausibly, this explained why he periodically retained meticulous records of the amount of cotton each slave picked. Cousin Ike later confirmed that Grandpa Bill spoke of how they were paid, but the amount they received was very small, before and after slavery, since they were easily enticed to migrate to Panola County, Mississippi for a better living.

Lemuel Reid's 1860 diary not only provided me with a snapshot of slave labor on the farm where Grandpa Bill was last enslaved, but it also dispelled some things I had believed about slavery. Also, many facets of American slavery that I was taught or had read were also confirmed in his diary. Having a false, preconceived notion that all slave-owners administered the orders while the enslaved laborers performed all of the work without monetary compensation, I shockingly surmised that Lemuel, as well as his sons and his mother, periodically worked with the slaves on a number of tasks. This was not only evident to me, but Wayne Reid noted:

Prior to reading Lemuel's diaries, I had always had the Hollywood stereotype impression of the southern planter, the master and family sat on the porch sipping Mint Juleps while the slaves did all of the manual labor. In reality, the operation more closely resembled a commune, as evidenced by the fact that even Lemuel's mother, who was 65 years old at the time, was picking cotton.[15]

During another one of my many conversations with Cousin Ike, he again relayed the story about Grandpa Bill and Lemuel Reid burying his gold during the Civil War, to hide them from pillaging Union soldiers. I had recently discovered that my maternal grandmother's maternal grandfather, Edward Danner, was a Union soldier who fought with the 59th Regiment Infantry of the United States Colored Troops (USCT). On July 17, 1862, Congress passed two acts that allowed for the enlistment of African-American men in Civil War service. However, official enrollment occurred after the Emancipation Proclamation of January 1, 1863, with General Order 143 issued by Edwin Stanton's War Department on May 22, 1863. This special order created the United States Colored Troops – a segregated army section for African-American Union regiments led by white officers. A total of 209,145 African-American men joined the USCT regiments, and somewhere between 38,000 and 68,000 African Americans inevitably lost their lives in America's bloodiest war.[16]

Curious if Grandpa Bill may have served in some capacity or may have had someone in his family to serve, I questioned, "Did Grandpa Bill talk about going to the War or knowing someone in his family who did?"

"He told me that he wanted to go to the War, but he was too young, and he wasn't allowed," Cousin Ike relayed confidently. Grandpa Bill Reed was around fourteen years old when the Civil War began in 1861. To enlist, soldiers had to be at least eighteen years old.

Cousin Ike continued, "He used to talk about how Lem Reid had sons who were killed in that War. I remember him telling me that."

"That is true," I responded, awestruck by the recollection of details. Before that conversation, I had never shared with him that Lemuel Reid, in fact, had two sons who perished in the Civil War. His eldest son, John White Reid (1841-1862), was fatally injured at the Battle

(4)

| | | | |
|---|---|---|---|
| Ben | 70 | 67 | 137 |
| Bill | 98 | 97 | 195 |
| Ann | 35 | 38 | 73 |
| Abram | 82 | 69 | 151 |
| Bob | 119 | 82 | 201 |
| Nat | 87 | 113 | 200 |
| Cal | 21 | 28 | 49 |
| Kate | 64 | 73 | 137 |
| Ples | 52 | | 52 |
| Leah | 82 | 75 | 157 |
| Israel | 137 | 92 | 229 |
| | | | 1581 |

One of several lists that Lemuel Reid kept to record the pounds of cotton that were picked by his slaves. This list is believed to be for the year 1860 or 1861.

of Mechanicsville, Virginia in June 1862, and died several days later in Richmond, Virginia. Another son, Samuel Orren Reid (1844-1862), who was known as "Bud," was obliterated by a cannon ball in that same battle. His body was never found.[17] Grandpa Bill and Bud had performed tasks together on the Reid Place shortly before he went off to the War. Slave-owners' children commonly developed friendships with young slaves on the plantation. As usual, Cousin Ike's memories of Grandpa Bill's stories of his time on the Reid Place were remarkably astounding.

Despite the sense of community that may have prevailed on the Reid Place and others, I unequivocally felt that Lemuel Reid, or any human being that enslaved other human beings and determined their destiny, were perpetuators of an inhumane yet lawful system that devastated my ancestors. They profited financially by their willingness to uphold the oppression of others by the racism – whether it was gentile or blatant – that governed their lives. However, only God can judge them. I welcomed the communication with Wayne Reid and other Reid descendants; they are responsible for their own lives and not Lemuel's. I greatly appreciated their willingness to share information since there were still so many descendants who hold the keys to unlock the gateway to the ancestral past of many African Americans but were and are unwilling to share the records of their slave-holding ancestors. Dorothy Spruill Redford so poignantly expressed the following shared thoughts in *Somerset Homecoming* to a descendant of her ancestors' enslaver:

> You inherit your ancestor's genes and their blood, but not
> their sins or their glories. If they did something wrong, if they
> lived a life that was stained, you carry forward a sense of guilt
> only if you're carrying the same attitudes. If the attitudes are
> gone, there is no need for the shame. That was yesterday, and
> this is today. Those were their lives, and these are ours . . .
> That we can live with the past without being dragged down

by it. That we cannot deny what happened here – that we must not deny it – and that we must restore this place to reflect all our histories.[18]

*This is an artistic description of a formerly enslaved African-American family working on a plantation shortly after Emancipation. This image was entitled "Plantation Scene - A Negro Hut," depicting the type of house many African-American families resided in during and after slavery. This house represents the type of dwelling that my ancestors probably were living in during slavery on the Barr and Reid farms in Abbeville County, South Carolina.*

*Source: "The Atlantic Slave Trade and Slave Life in the Americas: A Visual Record," (http://hitchcock.itc.virginia.edu/Slavery/index.php)*

# Chapter 5

## "They were his people."

ourt records of slave-owners have enabled many researchers to find enslaved ancestors. The Southern states contained more than four million enslaved African Americans in the South when the Civil War began in 1861. Only a small percentage of African-American families, especially in the South, were actually free before the Civil War. Estate records are the most valuable resources in tracing enslaved ancestors. They often contain the names of slaves frequently listed in wills and estate inventories. For that reason, I had to obtain the estate records for Rev. William H. Barr and Rebecca Reid Barr from the South Carolina Department of Archives and History (SCDAH) to try to uncover more about Pleasant Barr's history and the identity of Grandpa Bill Reed's mother. As Michael Barr indicated, Rev. Barr wrote a will that mentioned ten slaves. His will also indicated that he had more slaves. Who were in the "balance of negroes" that he bequeathed to his wife? I desperately wanted to know. Thankfully, the estate records were a genealogical goldmine.

Rather than planning a history-uncovering excursion to South Carolina to visit the SCDAH or the Abbeville County courthouse, for expediency I utilized the out-of-state research services offered by the SCDAH. Providing them with names, specific years of death, and a specific county where the deaths occurred, the archives assistant was able to locate the records for both Rev. William H. Barr and Rebecca Barr. They mailed to me a quote of the costs to obtain a copy of the files. I wrote a check and mailed the order form back to them on the same day. Little time was wasted.

As I waited for the records to arrive, I attempted to envision what it must have been like for Pleasant Barr to be forever separated from his wife, children, parents, and siblings; the imagined experience, that was truly the reality for many, was painful as I pictured myself being forcibly taken away from my own family. As I envisioned a scene of that gloomy day when brokenhearted Grandpa Bill watched his father being placed on James Giles's wagon, starring frozenly at the wagon as it rode off into the sunset, with tears running down his face, I wondered about the other family members that also witnessed this involuntary separation. Was Grandpa Bill's mother present? Who was she? Was there a cacophony of cries from her and Pleasant's own mother as he was being taken away? Who was his mother? What was her name? What happened to them? That nightmarish daydream lasted for several weeks.

The estate records arrived from the SCDAH four weeks later in a thick white envelope that was the key to unlocking the door to a difficult past. Rev. Barr wrote his will on Friday, January 6, 1843, three days before his death. Ill and feeble, the sixty-four-year-old Presbyterian minister anticipated his upcoming demise and made sure that his assets would be left to his wife and youngest children. The appraisers inventoried his estate on Friday, March 17, 1843. The inventory began with four cows and calves valued at twenty dollars and ended with human beings who were assigned a monetary value.

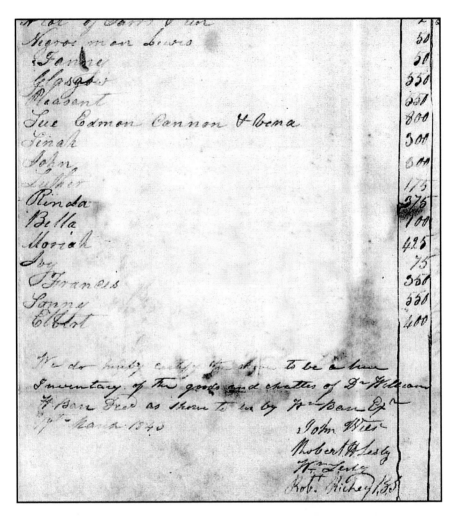

*Figure 5.1A. Slave inventory from the estate of Rev. William H. Barr, taken March 14, 1843*

| | |
|---|---|
| Negroe man Lewis | $50 |
| Fanny | $50 |
| Glasgow | $550 |
| Pleasant | $550 |
| Sue  Edmon  Cannon  Vena | $800 |
| Sinah | $300 |
| John | $300 |
| Luther | $175 |
| Rinda | $375 |
| Bella | $100 |
| Mariah | $425 |
| Ivy | $75 |
| Frances | $350 |
| Sonny | $550 |
| Elbert | $400 |

*Figure 5.1B. Slave inventory from the estate of Rev. William H. Barr, taken March 14, 1843*

Pleasant and seventeen others were listed by their names among Rev. Barr's four horses, twenty-nine sheep, one road wagon with a harness, farm equipment, carpenter tools, and a variety of other home and farming goods.

The discovery of this historical inventory was awe-inspiring. At the same time, I was heartbroken to see a monetary value placed beside their names. Forced servitude had been practiced in African and European countries before the transatlantic slave trade took a conservatively estimated 9.5 million African people to the Americas; however, it was not American plantation slavery or chattel slavery. Being able to maintain their identity, enslaved West Africans could own property, intermarry with the ruling class, and maintain a plethora of human rights that enslaved African Americans would never dream of having for over two hundred years. As I held the Barr slave inventory in my hands, the atrocity of American chattel slavery starred me directly in the face, and I saw a grim picture.

The day the inventory was taken was probably a very tense day for Pleasant and the rest of the Barr slaves, not knowing what would become of them since their "ole Masser" had died. Also, that day was likely a humiliating one, as they were in all probability examined like animals by the estate appraisers to determine their value. Slaves were often split apart after the demise of the slave-owner. Many were bequeathed to the slave-owner's children, grandchildren, nieces, or nephews who often migrated to other states. Some were sold at auctions to pay off debts and to settle the estate. Consequently, many family units were permanently broken. Born in 1849, William Anderson of Chickasaw County, Mississippi remembered:

"I has seed lots o' slaves auctioned off. Dey would put 'em up on a block, bidders would go examine dey teeth jus' like mules, make 'em dance an' prance 'round to see if dey was active. Dey was sol' to de highest bidders. Back den a good sound nigger would bring as high as $800."[1]

As I viewed the names of the others on the inventory, there was an overwhelming feeling that I was starring at the names of people whose blood flows through my veins. At the top of the slave listing were "Negro man Lewis" and Fanny. They were both appraised at $50, the lowest value given on the list. This signaled that they were the oldest enslaved adults on the Barr farm. Elderly slaves over the age of seventy were typically considered to be of zero value; therefore, a $50-value suggests that they were likely in their mid-50s to mid-60s. Pleasant retained the Barr name after slavery instead of keeping the Giles surname, signifying that he was likely born on Rev. Barr's farm in or around 1814. Many African-American men who opted to take the surname of a previous enslaver did so because of that reason. One of those men was Lewis Brown's father. The Arkansas ex-slave shared:

"My father was Lewis Bronson. He come from South Carolina . . . My father's owner was Elijah McCoy. Old Elijah McCoy was the owner, but they didn't take his name. They went back to the old standard mark after the surrender. They went back to the people where they come from, and they changed their names --- they changed off of them old names. McCoys was my masters, but my father went back to the name of the people way back over in South Carolina, where he come from. I don't know nothin' bout them."[2]

Since Pleasant was around twenty-nine years old at the time of the inventory, I immediately deduced that Lewis and Fanny may have been his parents and Grandpa Bill's paternal grandparents. However, would there be more clues to positively determine if they were an enslaved couple who bore children on the Barr farm? I was hopeful.

After Lewis and Fanny, the next two slaves listed on the inventory were Glasgow, oddly named after a city in Scotland, and Pleasant. They were both valued at $550. Were Glasgow and Rev. Glasgow Wilson one and the same person? Cousin Ike recalled that Rev. Glasgow Wilson and Grandpa Bill were closely related. Since Glasgow and Pleasant were given the same value, they were close in age, likely under five years apart. The 1880 U. S. Federal Census indicated that Rev. Glasgow Wilson was forty-six years old. The number may have come from Rev. Wilson himself or perhaps from a neighbor's guess, which meant that his birth year fell around, but not necessarily in, 1834. He would have been a young boy, under the age of ten, at the time of the inventory. Therefore, he was definitely not the one listed on the inventory.

Since fathers often had sons named after them, Glasgow appeared to have been the father of Rev. Glasgow Wilson, who may have been enslaved by Rebecca Barr's nephew-in-law, John R. Wilson. The Wilsons lived adjacent to Lemuel Reid and were also just a short distance from the Barr farm. If Glasgow and Pleasant were the sons of Lewis and Fanny, and if Rev. Glasgow Wilson was the son of Glasgow, then he and Grandpa Bill would have been first cousins. Since oral history confirmed a family relationship between them, would I be able to prove my theory?

Listed after Pleasant on the inventory were the names "Sue, Edmon, Cannon, Vena," who were all listed on one line and given one value of $800. This was a family. On slave inventories and appraisements, estate appraisers typically assigned one value to an enslaved female and her infant child or her youngest children who were under the age of five. Additional children born to the same mother were often listed afterwards in sequential order by age and/or monetary value. Through a methodical analysis, family relationships can often be determined with much certainty from slave inventories, facilitating the reconstruction of the family tree.[3]

Upon seeing the name Sue, who had a daughter named Vena, I immediately recalled the names that Grandpa Bill's sister, Mary, gave to her three children – Louvenia, Sue, and William. Vena was often a shorter name for Louvenia. Was Sue the wife of Pleasant and Grandpa Bill's mother? Or was Sue a sister of Pleasant and the daughter of Lewis and Fanny? The naming patterns were not a coincidence. During and after slavery, African Americans often named their children after family members, a cultural practice that can be traced back to West Africa. Irrefutably, there was a family connection to Sue and her children.

The time had come for me to drive down to Senatobia, Mississippi to visit with Cousin Ike again, to show him this monumental inventory. Maybe the names on the inventory may sound familiar. I sat down on his couch and began another revealing conversation.

"I have the inventory of the Barr farm where Grandpa Bill was first a slave. There were eighteen slaves on that place in 1843." I began to call out the names.

"Lewis, Fanny," I called. Cousin Ike said immediately, "Now, Grandpa Bill had a niece named Fanny."

"What," I said shockingly. "Yeah, we called her Aunt Fanny Key, but her name was Fanny McKee. She was married to Uncle Frank McKee. Grandpa told me that she was his niece, but I don't know if she was a sister's child or a brother's child. She came with them from South Carolina."

"Really," I said, still awed by the discovery of another relative. "Yes, she and Grandpa were close in age, so I don't know how she come to be his niece," Cousin Ike said in wonderment. This revelation later became another clue.

"Sue, Edmon, Cannon, Vena," I called out like a teacher taking roll. Cousin Ike's eyes lighted up like a Christmas tree, as he said, "I believe that was his brother!"

"Who?" I asked.

"Cannon," he said with excitement. "He talked about someone named Cannon all the time!"

"You're kidding, Cousin Ike," I said, amazed by yet another revelation. "No, I ain't. He and Cannon were close. He used to tell me about the things they used to do together growing up. But I believe Cannon and some others got taken away. He talked about how he waved goodbye to them, and he didn't see them anymore. Oh yes, Cannon had to have been his brother or something!"

I continued with the names, "Sina, John, Luther, Rinda, Bella, Mariah." Cousin Ike interrupted, "Mariah was his sister. He talked about her, too. I believe she was the one who raised him."

"Oh really?" I said. Still in awe, I continued, "Ivy, Frances, Sonny, and Elbert," pausing for a second between each name to see if other memories would be jarred.

"Yeah, many of those names sound familiar, but I definitely remember him talkin' 'bout Cannon and Mariah. They were his people. There's no doubt about that. How in the world did you find this slave list? This is something! I wonder what happened to them?"

Cousin Ike had wonderfully confirmed that the Barr slaves were Grandpa Bill's family members! This was a major breakthrough. However, was Sue his mother? Was her son, Cannon, his brother? Was she really his aunt? I knew that I needed to find more information to determine the exact family relationship between him and the Barr slaves. Sue was undoubtedly a close family member. Consequently, more unanswered questions surfaced.

Most of the eighteen Barr slaves, except Margaret Barr's slaves who were bequeathed to her, remained there on the Barr farm after 1843. Grandpa Bill was born approximately three years later. The 1850 slave schedule revealed that a number of others were also born on the Barr farm after 1843. It was the home of twenty-three enslaved people on December 14, 1850, the day they were counted by the federal government, but evidently deemed not human enough to have their names recorded in the slave schedules. William Jr. was the only son in Abbeville at the time. His father desired that he remained in Abbeville with his mother for awhile. Rev. Barr wrote in his will:

> . . . that my land whereon I now live, being composed of
> several small tracts, be divided by running a line as follows . .
> . and as I consider it very desirable that my son William
> should remain with his mother. I give and devise and
> bequeath all that tract lying on the west side of the line to my
> son William.

Honoring his father's wishes, William Jr. ran the small plantation with his mother Rebecca until he joined his older brother, Samuel McCorkle Barr, in Pontotoc County, Mississippi sometime before 1860.

During Grandpa Bill's childhood on the Barr farm, he most likely consumed the joys of childhood. The bondage of chattel slavery weighed carelessly on the shoulders of enslaved children. Having a father with a jovial personality, according to Cousin Ike, he was probably regaled with stories, songs, riddles, and playful banter, despite the ominous cloud of slavery that loomed over them. Like most other enslaved men, Pleasant seldom had special food or toys to share with him, and at times, he may have found it necessary to keep his children busy at chores and to teach them unsympathetic lessons of survival in a slave society. Presumably, by the age of eight, Grandpa

Bill began working intermittently at light tasks on the Barr farm, under the watchful eye of William Barr Jr. and Rebecca Barr. Children were typically set to work running errands, gathering wood, looking after babies and toddlers, or toting seeds.[4] Although they often had to perform such tasks for their owners during the day, children seldom worked for the duration of the day like adults. This left time for subsistence activities: feeding chickens and gathering eggs, tending rabbit traps, beating rice with a mortar and pestle, helping to cook, and performing a host of other chores.[5]

Rebecca Barr's estate record contained her will that she had written in 1861 and a small inventory. She died in January 1863, leaving all of her property to William Jr. On April 16, 1861, Rebecca instructed:

In the name of God, Amen! I Rebecca Barr of the District of Abbeville and State aforesaid, being of sound and disposing mind, memory, and understanding, desiring to dispose of my estate and property, do make and ordain this my last will and testament.
1. I will and direct that all my first debts be paid.
2. For divers good causes and considerations me hereunto moving, I give, desire and bequeath unto my son William Barr all of my estate and property of every nature and kind, and every interest that I possess or am legally or equitable entitled unto to him his heirs and (?) forever and I hereby appoint my son William executor of this will. In witness whereof I leave hereunto set my hand and seal this sixteenth day of April A. D. 1861.

The inventory of her estate, dated April 14, 1863, only reported two slaves, Glasgow, who was valued at $650, and Rinda, who was valued at $800. The words "not present" were in parenthesis besides Rinda's name. Where was Marinda? Interestingly, her nephew,

Lemuel Reid, was one of the estate appraisers. By this time, he was in possession of Grandpa Bill.

Although William Barr Jr. had settled in Pontotoc County, Mississippi, Glasgow was never taken away from Abbeville, as indicated by the 1870 and 1880 U. S. Federal Censuses. He, his wife, Rose, two sons, George and Oliver, and their wives and children were the only Barrs in Abbeville County. By 1863, most of the Barr slaves were apparently not in Rebecca Barr's possession and not in Abbeville County.

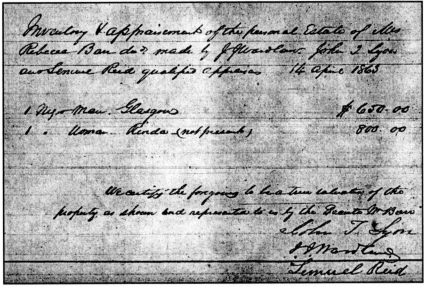

The inventory of Rebecca Reid Barr's estate, taken April 14, 1863, listed only Glasgow and Rinda. Besides Rinda's name was the notation "not present."

An artistic painting entitled "Slaves Waiting for Sale, Richmond, Virginia, 1861," painted by Eyre Crowe and published in Hugh Honour, The Image of the Black in Western Art (Menil Foundation, Harvard University Press, 1989), vol. 4, pt. 1, p. 205, fig. 127 Source: "The Atlantic Slave Trade and Slave Life in the Americas: A Visual Record," (http://hitchcock.itc.virginia.edu/Slavery/index.php)

# Chapter 6

## The Mysterious Mother

No one recalled anything that was said about Grandpa Bill Reed's mother. I found that to be quite unusual. Cousin Ike Deberry did not remember anything, and Uncle Jimmy Reed, Grandpa Bill's first born, obviously did not know her name since "not known" were written on Grandpa Bill's death certificate. My mother and I have such a close relationship that I could not imagine that anyone, who knows me well, would not have heard me say anything about her. During a time when many enslaved families were torn apart, the bonds between mothers and children were certainly cherished. Since the only memory of Grandpa Bill's parentage involved his father and a motherly older sister, perhaps his mother was one of the family members who were taken away. Maybe it was simply too painful for Grandpa Bill to share many details about her. Meticulously, I attempted to uncover her identity based on the information that was unearthed thus far.

The family oral history established that Grandpa Bill Reed was born on the Barr farm, where he watched his father being sold away.

| ID # | Age | Sex | Color | Who were they? | Owner |
|------|-----|-----|-------|----------------|-------|
| 1 | 35 | Male | B | Pleasant | Wm Barr, Jr. |
| 2 | 25 | Male | B | Sawney | "    " |
| 3 | 23 | Female | B | Mariah | Margaret Barr |
| 4 | 6 | Female | Mu | daughter of Mariah | "    " |
| 5 | 5 | Female | B | daughter of Mariah | "    " |
| 6 | 3 | Male | B | son of Mariah | "    " |
| 7 | 18 | Male | B | Elbert | "    " |
| 8 | 16 | Female | B | Sina | "    " |
| 9 | 50 | Female | B | Bella | Rebecca Barr |
| 10 | 4 | Male | B | **Matches Grandpa Bill** | "    " |
| 11 | 38 | Male | B | Glasgow | "    " |
| 12 | 35 | Male | B | Pleasant ** | "    " |
| 13 | 36 | Female | B | Sue | "    " |
| 14 | 11 | Male | B | Edmond | "    " |
| 15 | 9 | Male | Mu | Cannon | "    " |
| 16 | 7 | Female | Mu | Louvenia | "    " |
| 17 | 6 | Male | Mu | son of Sue | "    " |
| 18 | 5 | Male | Mu | son of Sue | "    " |
| 19 | 3 | Male | Mu | son of Sue | "    " |
| 20 | 1 | Male | Mu | son of Sue | "    " |
| 21 | 34 | Female | B | Marinda | "    " |
| 22 | 8 | Male | Mu | son of Marinda | "    " |
| 23 | 65 | Female | B | Fanny | "    " |

*Table 6.1. The slaves on the Barr farm, taken from the 1850 Slave Schedule, Abbeville County, South Carolina (**The census-taker appeared to have counted Pleasant Barr twice.)*

Who were the females enslaved on the Barr farm in or around 1846? Fortunately, I had the 1843 inventory, although it was taken about three years before Grandpa Bill's birth. With reasonable certainty, one of the women on that inventory had to be his mother. This was so because a slave's status was determined by the status of the mother. If an African-American woman was free, all of her children were free. If an enslaved woman had children by a free African-American man, her children were also enslaved. Which one was his mother?

Determined to unearth something about this mysterious mother, I compared the nameless data in the 1850 Abbeville County Slave Schedule for the Barrs to the 1843 inventory and Rev. William H. Barr's will. This enabled me to place a name with the slaves counted on the Barr farm in 1850. Unlike the census-takers, I gave them an identity, and the identity of Grandpa Bill's mother was paramount to his history – she gave him life.

The enslaved human bodies counted for William Barr Jr. and Margaret Barr were irrefutably the ones that their father had bequeathed to them in 1843 (see table 6.1). In Rev. Barr's will, he left Pleasant and Sawney to William Jr. He left Mariah, Sina, and Elbert to Margaret. Therefore, in table 6.1, slave #1 and slave #2, who were owned by William Jr., were Pleasant and Sawney. Slave #3, who was owned by Margaret, was Mariah. The three young children listed after her, slaves #4, #5, and #6, were unquestionably her children. Fortunately, the census-taker who visited the Barr farm conveniently grouped slaves by family groups, mother and children. This was signaled by much younger slaves recorded after an adult female. This assisted my ancestral search. Regardless of the helpful way he reported mothers with their children, I was still disheartened by the omission of names in these records. Nonetheless, slaves #7 and #8, the last two slaves listed for Margaret Barr, were undoubtedly Elbert and Sina.

Rev. Barr had also given Frances, John, and Luther to his daughter, Elizabeth. However, Elizabeth was not found in the 1850 slave schedule. The remaining slaves were the legal property of Rebecca. Rev. Barr instructed, "The balance of my negroes I give desire and bequeath to my wife for and during her life or widowhood and at the happening of either of these events the same to be equally divided amongst my children with by sale or other means as shall seem proper to a majority of my children." When Rebecca's father, Hugh Reid, died in 1829, she inherited a slave girl named Marinda, per the instructions of his will. Rev. Barr requested in his will that "Rinda" remained her property, and he also bequeathed Glasgow to her. The residual slaves that she now possessed were Lewis, Fanny, Sue and her children Edmon, Cannon, Louvenia, and Bella. Any children born to the women would also become her legal property during her life or widowhood. They all comprised of slaves #9 to #23, a total of fifteen slaves. Which one was Grandpa Bill's mother? Fortunately, there were clues – a preponderance of circumstantial evidence.

**Clue 1:**

Since Grandpa Bill Reed was born on the Barr farm, one of the young males counted in the 1850 slave schedule was certainly him. He was around three or four years old; therefore, three young males were considered: slave #6, slave #10, and slave #19. Which one was Grandpa Bill?

Slave #6 was a three-year-old son of Mariah. Cousin Ike remembered that Mariah was Grandpa Bill's sister. Thus, slave #6 was a nephew and immediately ruled out.

Slave #19 was a three-year-old son of Sue. A number of Sue's children were reported as mulatto (Mu). In all probability, her children were of light complexion and were probably fathered by either a white man or an enslaved mulatto man who lived on a nearby plantation. Although the term mulatto meant that a slave had a black parent and a white parent, census-takers often based the color designation on appearances rather than actual parentage. A light-skinned, enslaved African American could have had either two mulatto parents, one mulatto parent and a black parent, or a black parent and a white parent. Grandpa Bill was not light complexioned, according to his grandchildren, or a mulatto, as his father was Pleasant. Therefore, Sue could not have been his mother or the wife of Pleasant. Slave #19 was then ruled out. Nevertheless, because Cousin Ike recalled from Grandpa Bill's stories that his beloved companion Cannon was a close relative, this suggested that he and Grandpa Bill were not brothers but more likely first cousins.

Slave #10, the last enslaved youth in question, was obviously the young son of slave #9, a fifty-year-old female. She was most probably Bella, since she was appraised at a low value of $100 in 1843. Was Bella the mysterious mother?

| MALE SLAVES | | FEMALE SLAVES | |
|---|---|---|---|
| Age 0 – 14 | Age 27 – 45 | Age 0 – 14 | Age 27 – 45 |
| 3 | 1 | 1 | 1 |

Table 6.2. The 1820 Census of Abbeville County, South Carolina – Rev. William Barr's slave-holdings

| MALE SLAVES | | | FEMALE SLAVES | | |
|---|---|---|---|---|---|
| Under Age 10 | Age 10 – 24 | Age 36 – 55 | Under Age 10 | Age 10 – 24 | Age 36 – 55 |
| 3 | 2 | 1 | 2 | 3 | 1 |

Table 6.3. The 1830 Census of Abbeville County, South Carolina – Rev. William Barr's slave-holdings

**Clue 2:**

Interestingly, earlier census records also aided in this ancestral search, despite containing only statistical information. At this point, I wanted to investigate all records possible to pinpoint my great-great-grandmother. In the 1820 U. S. Federal Census of Abbeville County, Rev. Barr was reported as having only six slaves (see table 6.2). It was the first census that listed the number of male and female slaves by age group. The prior censuses only recorded the number of slaves a person owned. Two of Rev. Barr's six slaves were an adult male and an adult female, who were between twenty-seven and forty-five years old. With much certainty, the two adults were Lewis and Fanny, who were the oldest slaves on the Barr farm in 1843. The four remaining slaves were youths, three males and one female, who were between zero and fourteen years old. The age difference clearly indicate that the six slaves were likely one family unit that contained four children – Glasgow, Pleasant, Sue, who were all under the age of ten, and another young boy.

By 1830, the Barr farm gained two female slaves to labor without compensation. In the 1830 U. S. Federal Census, two additional females were counted in the 10-24 age column. They were not accounted for in 1820 (see table 6.3). Rebecca Barr inherited Marinda from her father's estate in 1829; therefore, she accounts for one of them. Marinda had only one child in 1850, an eight-year-old mulatto son. She could not have been Grandpa Bill's mother. This too left Bella as the one in question. Hence, in the 1820s, Rev. Barr acquired yet another female slave who was most probably Bella and not blood-related to Pleasant.

## Clue 3:

As I analyzed my findings, more evidence pinpointed Bella as being the likely maternal candidate. Grandpa Bill told his family that Fanny McKee was his niece, although everyone called her "Aunt Fanny." She was found in the 1870, 1880, 1900, and 1910 U. S. Federal Census of Panola County, Mississippi. South Carolina was consistently reported as her birthplace. Based on her ages reported in the census records, her birth year fell around 1848. Cousin Ike was accurate in his assessment that she and Grandpa Bill were close in age. Since he had a niece who was born within two years after his birth, he obviously had a much older sibling. Thus, Grandpa Bill was likely not born to a very young mother. The average age an enslaved mother gave birth to her first child was between seventeen and nineteen years old. Since his sister Mariah was listed after Bella on the 1843 inventory, indicating that they were likely mother and daughter, Bella and Mariah matched this situation.

In 1850, Bella was reported as being nearly fifty years old with a four-year-old son. Her age was estimated in the slave schedule since a number divisible by five was recorded. Enslaved women bearing children well into their late forties was not uncommon. The 1850 slave schedule also shows that Mariah had children in the same age range as Grandpa Bill. Unfortunately, Cousin Fanny McKee's 1928 death certificate did not contain her parents' names. The informant, Uncle Jimmy Reed, lacked that knowledge. However, she was probably the daughter of Mariah.

Why didn't Mariah come to Mississippi with Grandpa Bill and the others? Did she remain in Abbeville? Did she die before slavery ended? What happened to Bella? Was she sold away too after 1850 like Pleasant? Did she die shortly after 1850 when Grandpa Bill was still a child? Or was she the one who died in Alabama while they were migrating to Mississippi after slavery? The whereabouts of Bella, Mariah, and the rest of the Barr slaves were indeed a mystery. Viewing the Barr slave inventory periodically, I often wondered and shouted, "What happened to them!" Despite the frustration, I remained confident. I knew that one day I would find them.

Five generations of one family on Smith's plantation, Beaufort, South Carolina, photograph by Timothy H. O'Sullivan, Image Reference NW0243, as shown on www.slaveryimages.org, sponsored by the Virginia Foundation for the Humanities and the University of Virginia Library.

# Chapter 7

## What happened to them?

After slavery, many freed African Americans sought diligently to locate family members from whom they were forcibly separated. Many walked miles of roadways, placed numerous newspaper advertisements, and spent any money that they had attempting to reunite with their mothers, fathers, wives, children, siblings, and others. Freedmen Bureau records contain many requests like that of Texas resident, Hawkins Wilson, who had been sold away from his family in Virginia. On May 11, 1867, he requested, "I am anxious to learn about my sisters, from whom I have been separated many years – I have never heard from them since I left Virginia twenty four years ago. I am in hopes that they are still living and I am anxious to hear how they are getting on . . ."[1]

Fortunately, many African Americans were able to reunite with their families. As author, John Baker Jr., disclosed in *The Washingtons of Wessyngton Plantation*, his ten-year-old great-great-grandfather, Thomas Black Cobb of Robertson County, Tennessee, was sold away from his mother, brothers, and sisters in 1854 in the settlement of the estate. Remarkably, he was able to reunite with his family after slavery.[2] Unfortunately, the majority of former slaves who actively sought their families were unsuccessful. Grandpa Bill Reed had a younger sister, a niece, and a first cousin who came with him to Mississippi after slavery, but he never reunited with a plethora of other family members, including his parents. I could not help but wonder what happened to them. I was determined to find out.

Before there was online access to census records, researchers had to scroll through seemingly miles of microfilmed census records to locate people of the past. Since William Barr Jr. had settled in Pontotoc County, Mississippi sometime before 1860, I searched there exhaustively for Grandpa Bill's family. So, I thought. Assuming that they retained the Barr surname after slavery, like Pleasant and Glasgow had done, I browsed the 1870 census index book for Mississippi, which list the heads of households. Through the glare of the microfilm machine, I also browsed the 1880 soundex for any Barrs in Pontotoc County. A soundex is a phonetic index that was generated based on the sound of the surname. It had to be utilized first to know exactly where to find people in the census records by the county, enumeration district number, and the census sheet number. It is available only for the 1930, 1920, 1910, 1900, and 1880 censuses.

Sawney Barr was the only one found in Pontotoc County, residing in the town of Pontotoc. Where were the rest of them? His age was reported as being forty-one, and in his household were presumably his wife, Caroline, thirty-five years old, and two teenage children, Frank, age sixteen, and Anna, age fourteen. According to the Mississippi Historical Society, Sawney had been a blacksmith who worked in a blacksmith shop in the town of Pontotoc, shoeing horses for both the Union and Confederate Armies during the Civil War.[3] After slavery, he became a prominent figure in the county during Reconstruction (1865-1876).

Amazingly, Sawney was recorded in Pontotoc County's history as the First Superintendent of Education for Pontotoc County.[4] Following the South's defeat in the Civil War, the pro-slavery government of Mississippi was replaced by a reconstructed government with the assistance of the Union Army. The Fourteenth Amendment of the United States Constitution ushered in another change in Mississippi, not allowing politicians to refuse to pledge allegiance to the Union. Consequently, a number of African Americans entered positions in state government and on school boards, and a large number of African-American children entered schools. However, the political gains of African Americans during Reconstruction would soon be wiped out. The racist Klu Klux Klan increased their reign of terrorism across the South during the 1870s, and many African Americans were forcibly ousted from these important positions. Unfortunately, the Old South had risen again.

Sawney was not located in any censuses after 1870, suggesting that he may have died or left Mississippi after the Klu Klux Klan's violent missions. Other than Pleasant Barr, who was in Tippah County, I could not locate anyone else in the 1870 census index and the 1880 soundex. Why weren't they there? The 1860 U. S. Federal Census of Pontotoc County enumerated William Barr in the county, and he was the owner of seventeen enslaved laborers (see table 7.1). Did those seventeen slaves not contain the slaves once owned by his parents? Other than Sawney, who was bequeathed to him in 1843, did William acquire new slaves after migrating to Mississippi? Finding only Sawney in Pontotoc County seemed puzzling.

For over two years, I wondered about the whereabouts of the other Barr slaves. Surely, all of them did not perish during slavery. Somebody has to be somewhere. But, where? Perhaps, after they were emancipated, they relocated to another state and took another surname. Although many slaves opted to remain in the same area where they had been enslaved, many decided to start a new life far away from the county where they had lived through slavery, like Grandpa Bill Reed had done. He migrated over six hundred miles to northern Mississippi. Maybe Fanny, if she had survived slavery, Sue,

Edmond, Cannon, Vena, Bella, and Marinda migrated to Tennessee, Arkansas, Alabama, or maybe to places further north. Again, assuming that they retained the Barr surname, I checked a number of state census indexes for 1870, only to be met with disappointment. I could not find them. Nevertheless, something would not let me give up the search. My hope never waned.

Finally, in 2001, advancement in technology provided more hope for locating them. During the spring of that year, the Church of Jesus Christ of Latter-day Saints, also known as the Mormon Church, announced the release of the 1880 U. S. Census Records on CD-ROM, a monumental new database to assist researchers in locating people in the 1880 census. The microfilmed 1880 soundex only contain families with at least one child who was ten years old or younger. It was initially created in 1935, not for genealogy purposes, but to provide birth information for the newly-created Social Security System. Individuals in 1935, who were fifty-five to sixty-five years old, would have been ten years old or younger in 1880; therefore, the soundex provided another check to confirm a person's age. Because of this limitation, many people in the 1880 census were not located, not because they were not recorded by a census-taker, but because their household did not contain a child who was ten years old and younger.

Amazingly, the 1880 U. S. Census CD-ROM database contain approximately 50 million individuals. Hundreds of volunteers had dedicated many hours transcribing the microfilmed 1880 census records of all the states and then typed the information into the new database. The transcribed records contain each person's last name, first name, age, sex, race, marital status, occupation, relationship to the head of household, state or country of birth, father's state or country of birth, mother's state or country of birth, as well as the National Archives microfilm number and page number, and the Family History Library microfilm number. What was even more spectacular was that the CD-ROM set contain a search engine. I was ecstatic about its release.

Perhaps, this new technology would enable me to locate more of Grandpa Bill's family. I anxiously awaited for my order to arrive.

Finally, on the evening of Wednesday, August 15, 2001, I arrived home from a busy day at work to find my 1880 Census CD-ROM set on my doorstep. I was astounded at the extensiveness of the database. It contained fifty-six CD-ROM disks with a nice three-ring binder to store the massive collection. One CD-ROM disk only weighs about a half-ounce, and the binder with all the 1880 census disks inside weighs several pounds.

After opening the package and installing the viewer on my computer, I retrieved the disk that contains the B surnames to commence my search for my missing family. In the search engine, I typed "Barr" for the last name, "Pontotoc" for the county, and "Mississippi" for the state. I was awestruck at what popped up on the computer screen!

Low and behold, the search results contained Fannie Barr, who was reported as being one hundred years old, and Isabella Barr, who was reported as sixty-five years old. My heart pounded rapidly as I began to realize that my prayers had been answered. I finally located my family. Fanny, who was given a $50 value in 1843 because of her advanced age, was still living as late as 1880. If I had done the eye-weary and time-consuming task of scrolling the 1880 Pontotoc County census line by line, I would have found them several years ago. Nonetheless, William Barr Jr. had, in fact, taken Grandpa Bill's suspected mother Bella, Fanny, and Sawney to Pontotoc County with him. Where were the others?

Interestingly, Fanny Barr, who was born in Virginia, was living in the household of someone named Jacob Beckley, who was born in South Carolina. She was reported as being his grandmother. Isabella Barr was living in the household of someone named Henry Clay Beckley and was reported as being his aunt.

"Who in the world are these Beckleys," I questioned loudly as my eyes penetrated the computer screen. The names Jacob and Henry Clay were unfamiliar to me.

To see if other Beckleys resided in Pontotoc County, I inputted the surname and its variant spellings in the search engine. Low and behold, the following three names appeared: Cannon Beckley, who was recorded on page 108D, the same page Jacob Beckley and Fanny Barr were found, Edmond Beckley, who was recorded on page 86D, and Lewis Beckley, who was recorded on page 96C.

I bawled instantly, "That's Edmond and Cannon! Oh my God! I found them!"

This burst of excitement was followed by a happy dance in my bedroom. I was consumed with joy. Indeed, they were right there in Pontotoc County, too. I had missed them because I erroneously assumed that they would have retained the Barr surname.

"Why did they take the Beckley surname instead of Barr," I again questioned loudly as I sat back down at the computer to gather my thoughts. The only other time I had ever heard of this surname was in reference to Beckley, West Virginia.

As I studied the 1880 Pontotoc County census, the genealogical puzzle of my Barr family members was pieced together. The census taker reported Edmond, Cannon, Jacob, Lewis, and Henry Clay Beckley's color as mulatto. South Carolina was reported as their birthplace. Evidently, they were the sons of Sue, since most of her children's color was reported as mulatto in the 1850 Abbeville County Slave Schedule. Jacob, Henry Clay, and Lewis Beckley were born to Sue after the 1843 slave inventory was taken. Perhaps, the Beckley surname was the surname of their father. Who was he? Where was he? Was he a white man or was he a mulatto man who chose the Beckley surname? Where was Sue?

Additionally, the 1870 census revealed that Sue's sons lived on William Barr's plantation that year, just five years after slavery. Isabella, whose name was inaccurately spelled "Isalla" by the census-taker, was also among them. Interestingly, her age was reported as seventy. Marinda Barr was reported as a black, fifty-five-year-old cook in William's household.

Amazingly, finding Sue's sons provided further proof that Rev. Barr's oldest slaves, Lewis and Fanny, were, in fact, an enslaved couple who bore children – Glasgow, Pleasant, Sue, and likely others, including Sawney. More wonderfully, they were my great-great-great-grandparents. That was going back five generations! Fanny was the confirmed grandmother of Sue's children, and Sue had named one of her sons after Lewis. A common practice was naming African-American children after their grandparents.

Since Rev. Barr was a minister, he may have allowed Lewis and Fanny to "jump the broom into holy matrimony," a common practice among enslaved African Americans whose marriages were not sanctioned by law. He may have even performed the ceremony. One can surmise that their enslavement on his small farm may not have been as strict as many others who endured unkind enslavers. Perhaps, they were already a married couple when he acquired them. Many slave-owners supported and often encouraged slaves to find mates, as it typically resulted in lucrative procreation. Enslaved African-American families were often large, and each birth of a child that survived infancy increased the wealth of the slave-owner. Moreover, some slave-owners believed that enslaved men with families would become more docile and less susceptible to running away.

Since Isabella Barr was reported as being Henry Clay Beckley's aunt, this census finding added to the preponderance of circumstantial evidence that Bella was likely the wife or mate of his uncle, Pleasant, and the mother of Grandpa Bill Reed. Why did the Barrs separate Pleasant and Isabella? To add more insult to injury, why did they separate Isabella from her children? How could they have been so merciless?

Thankfully, Isabella was able to be among family fifteen years after slavery. She had not seen Grandpa Bill in twenty years and would never see him again. The Barrs' decisions regarding their slaves represented the inhumane actions of many slave-owners. Mothers were separated from children, husbands from wives, sisters from brothers, fathers from sons, grandparents from grandchildren, and the list goes on. The permanent disruption of many enslaved families was, without a doubt, one of the most pernicious aspects of American slavery. Many African Americans today are unknowingly blood relatives, and many of these consanguineous connections may never be uncovered.

Shortly after this startling discovery, the death certificates of Sue's sons, Jacob and Lewis, were located at the MDAH. At the age of seventy, Rev. Jacob C. Beckley had died in 1917 in Marshall County, Mississippi. He was just thirty miles from Grandpa Bill. Lewis Beckley's death occurred in 1942 in Pontotoc County, at the age of around 93 of chronic cardiac failure. On Lewis's death record, only the mother's name was reported – Susie Beckley. The informant, M. J. Beckley, did not know his father's name. On Jacob's death record, the father's name was reported as being Jacob Beckley, and the mother's maiden name was reported as "Susan ----." The informant, Lary Moore, appeared to have known a little about him but only had knowledge of his mother's first name. Rev. Jacob C. Beckley had been a minister in Holly Springs, the home of Rust College. Even more revealing, his birthplace was recorded as "Abeville, South Carolina." This was the only death certificate out of many found throughout my research that recorded the town and the state of birth. The rest only contained the state of birth.

I researched the census records again to see what else I could find. Where were Jacob and Sue Beckley? Did they have any more children? Fortunately, that search was fruitful. Sue and four of her children resided in and near Oxford, Mississippi in Lafayette County, which was Pontotoc County's neighbor to the west. A distance of thirty-five miles separated the towns of Oxford and Pontotoc. Recorded as "S. Beckley" in the 1880 census, Sue was a resident nurse in the household of William S. Pettus, who was a town merchant. Interestingly, William's cousin, Mississippi Governor John Jones Pettus, played a significant role in directing the state to follow South Carolina's succession from the Union on January 9, 1861. Also, another cousin, Alabama Senator Edmund Pettus, was the politician for whom the infamous Highway 80 Bridge over the Alabama River into Selma, Alabama was named for. The Edmund Pettus Bridge was the site of the conflict of Bloody Sunday on March 7, 1965, when armed white officers attacked a group of peaceful Civil Rights demonstrators with clubs and tear gas.

Additionally, the 1880 census-taker reported Sue's age as being sixty-eight, and her birthplace was recorded as being South Carolina. Whether or not this information was given by Sue herself is conjecture; however, this census report and her reported age in the 1850 slave schedule indicate that she was born sometime between 1812 and 1814 and was just a year or two older than her brother, Pleasant. Also, in 1880, her oldest son, John Beckley, who was given a value of $300 on the 1843 Barr inventory, was reported as a resident, unmarried servant in the household of Hugh Alexander Barr. Hugh was the older brother of William Barr Jr. The second oldest son of Rev. William and Rebecca Barr, he had become a prominent lawyer in Oxford during slavery. The following excerpt from an 1899 memorial address, delivered by Judge Lumsford P. Cooper to the Bar Association of Lafayette County shortly after his death, gave a snapshot of his life:

> H. A. was born in Abbeville, S. C. in October, 1816. When he first grew up he emigrated to the West on horseback, and stopped at the city of Columbus, in Mississippi, where he sought and obtained employment as a Clerk for several years. From there he went to Oxford in 1843 and studied law with his brother (James), and, after obtaining his license, he returned to South Carolina to visit his mother, his father having died in the meantime. About this time he became a

member of the Presbyterian Church, and was a devout and
regular attendant upon that church to day of his death . . .
After visiting his mother, he, on horseback, rode through
Florida, and perhaps a portion of Alabama, seeking a location
for the practice of his profession. He finally landed at Oxford
in 1845, and went into the office of his brother, who was then
living, and continued the practice in partnership with his
brother until 1849, when his brother died. From that time
until his death, he continued the practice in the same office
and justly deserved as he had by patient industry and
studious habits the reputation of being, as he was, one of the
most accurate, painstaking and faithful lawyers in North
Mississippi . . .[5]

Hugh Barr was on the Executive Committee of the Board of
Trustees at the University of Mississippi until 1882. He was also a
lecturer of law at the university.[6] In 1929, a newly constructed
residence hall on campus was named for him. Renovated in 1976 to an
academic facility, Barr Hall now houses the Department of Music and
the African-American Studies Program, an academic unit of the
College of Liberal Arts that was implemented in 1970. I find it rather
ironic that the African-American Studies Program at Ole Miss, the
common nickname for the university, would be housed in a building
that was named after a man whose family owned slaves – my ancestors
– and separated some of them from their own families before the Civil
War.

A search in the Lafayette County marriage and census records
revealed the identity of two additional daughters of Sue, named Patsy
and Susie, and confirmed the identity of another daughter, Sina. Susie
Beckley married Simon Sheegog on January 11, 1876, and Patsy Beckley
married John Saddler on Christmas Day of that same year. Both
couples married in Lafayette County and were also located in that
county in 1880 and 1900. Patsy and Susie had been born to Sue circa

1855 and 1857, respectively, on the Barr farm near Abbeville, South Carolina. They were just toddlers when they were transported in wagons to northern Mississippi. However, they were cognizant of their birthplace since South Carolina was reported to the census-takers as being their state of birth.

In 1900, just two households away from the Sheegogs, lived Sam and Sina Williamson, ages sixty-eight and sixty-seven, respectively. Sina Williamson's death certificate confirmed that she was the daughter of Sue Beckley. Like Lewis's death record, the informant did not know her father's name. However, she named one of her sons Jacob, providing evidence that her father was likely Jacob Beckley as well. She was "Sina," who Rev. William Barr had bequeathed to his daughter, Margaret, and "Sinah," who was valued at $300 on the 1843 Barr inventory. The Williamsons relocated to Lafayette County, Mississippi in the 1870s, obviously to be near Sina's mother and her siblings, John, Patsy, and Susie.

Was Hugh Barr the reason why Sue and her children were in Lafayette County? Were they transferred to Hugh after his younger brother William had transported them to Mississippi? If so, when? Perhaps, this occurred shortly before the Civil War began in 1861.

The 1860 Pontotoc County slave schedule suggests that they were owned by William Barr Jr. that year, since many of his slaves closely matched their approximated ages and sex (see table 7.1). How often did Sue and her children travel to Pontotoc County to visit with her mother Fanny and her sons, Edmond, Cannon, Jacob, Henry Clay, and Lewis Beckley? Did she even know that when her brother, Pleasant, was sold to James Giles and was taken away from South Carolina, he was taken to Ripley, just forty-five miles northeast of her? Did Fanny ever learn that her son Pleasant was just forty miles away from her when William brought her to Pontotoc County? Obviously, Grandpa Bill Reed never knew that his father, suspected mother, grandmother, aunt, uncles, and many cousins, including his beloved childhood companion, Cannon, were right there in northern Mississippi too, just under one hundred miles away from the Old Home Place. Sadly, they were so close but yet so far because of slavery's inhumanities.

| ID # | AGE | SEX | COLOR | WHO WERE THEY? |
|------|-----|-----|-------|----------------|
| 1 | 66 | Female | B | Fanny |
| 2 | 52 | Male | Mu | Jacob Sr. |
| 3 | 45 | Female | B | Isabella |
| 4 | 44 | Female | B | Sue |
| 5 | 43 | Female | B | Marinda |
| 6 | 30 | Male | B | Sawney |
| 7 | 26 | Female | B | ? |
| 8 | 22 | Male | B | Edmond |
| 9 | 20 | Male | B | Cannon |
| 10 | 18 | Female | B | Louvenia |
| 11 | 16 | Male | B | Henry Clay |
| 12 | 14 | Male | B | Jacob Jr. |
| 13 | 12 | Male | B | Lewis |
| 14 | 9 | Male | B | Joseph |
| 15 | 7 | Female | B | ? |
| 16 | 5 | Female | B | Patsy |
| 17 | 3 | Female | B | Susie |

Table 7.1. The slaves on William Barr's plantation in Pontotoc County, Mississippi, taken from the 1860 Slave Schedule, Pontotoc County, Mississippi

# Chapter 8

## More Revelations

When I entered into the addictive world of genealogy, I learned a lot more about African-American history that surprised me. One of many interesting facts that I learned was that a number of enslaved African Americans, especially house servants, were often permitted or required to worship at their enslaver's church. Many of them were even baptized in those churches, and their membership and baptisms were often recorded in church minutes. Surviving church records are one of many genealogical resources that researchers can explore and are often omitted. Since the enslaver of my Barr ancestors was a Presbyterian minister, perhaps Lewis, Fanny, Glasgow, Pleasant, Sue, Isabella, and the rest were members of the Upper Long Cane Presbyterian Church, where Rev. William H. Barr had been a minister for thirty-three years. I wondered.

Fortunately, I had been communicating online with John Blythe, an Abbeville resident and a member of the Abbeville Historical Society. He was keenly interested in the research of my enslaved ancestors in

Abbeville County. His love of history and his understanding of the difficulty of slave ancestral research led him to visit the church to see what records may exist that may have recorded any slave members, hopefully my ancestors. I was extremely grateful for his genealogical act of kindness.

John did not waste any time checking out this potentially informative resource. Within twenty-four hours of corresponding with him, he e-mailed, "Melvin, I went to Upper Long Cane Church this morning and looked at the Session books. A list of 'Coloured Members' exceeds 150, and there is a separate section for baptized persons (infants, etc.). In the meantime, I took some notes to pass along. Some of these fit right in to what you know. Others threw me off, but may make sense to you . . . The earliest Session book covers the period 1852-1869."[1] Several days later, I received a thick brown envelope in the mail. John had photocopied the entries from the church's Session book that recorded the slaves. The church records were a goldmine.

Most of the Barr slaves had joined Upper Long Cane Church during the 1850s. They were not members during a time when Rev. Barr was the pastor, from 1809 to 1843. This served to my advantage since the Session book for that time period was forever lost. Did Rev. Barr not permit his slaves to attend the church? If not, why? I wondered.

However, the most mind-boggling question that was more perplexing to me than any others about him was – how did he justify being a minister of the Gospel who supported the enslavement of God's human creation. Not only that, he permitted the splitting of families, as evident in his will when he instructed, "The balance of my negroes I give & bequeath to my wife for and during her life or widowhood and at the happening of either of these events the same to be equally divided amongst my children either by sale or other means as shall seem proper to a majority of my children."

*Upper Long Cane Presbyterian Church, Abbeville, South Carolina, as it appeared when Rev. William H. Barr was pastor, from 1809 to 1843. Source: "Keeping the Faith, A History of Upper Long Cane Presbyterian Church"*

Suddenly, the thought came to me. My ancestors were not considered human – not enough for their names to be written in slave schedules but yet considered as monetary value like cattle, hogs, and other livestock. Many people justified in their minds the enslavement of people who were considered to be animals. Nonetheless, I will forever be dumbfounded by the fact that Rev. Barr and others participated in the atrocious institution of chattel slavery and regarded themselves as devout Christians at the same time. To me, this contradicted the very nature of God, and it upheld the hypocritical mindset of the time.

Rev. Barr obtained a Doctor of Divinity degree from Franklin College in Athens, Georgia in 1824. He was a slave-owner of my ancestors by this time. All of the published sources that I read about him conveniently overlooked the fact that he was a Presbyterian minister who owned slaves – whose blood I carry. He was not alone. During slavery, the Presbyterian Church was starkly divided on the issue. Many Presbyterians, especially in the northern colonies, considered slavery to be a moral problem. As early as 1787, the Synod of Philadelphia and New York urged its members to progressively bring an end to slavery. Later, in 1818, the Presbyterian General Assembly condemned slavery as "a gross violation of the most precious and sacred rights of human nature" that contradicted God's law.[2] However, many southern Presbyterians like Rev. Barr defended the peculiar institution. They considered it as an economic and political problem rather than a spiritual one.[3] Despite his stance on slavery, Rev. Barr was praised by many, including Alexander Bowie of Talledega, Alabama, who expressed the following details in 1849:

*My acquaintance with him commenced near the close of the year 1809. About that time, on my return from College, I found him in charge of the Upper Long Cane Presbyterian Church, near the village of Abbeville in South Carolina. I shall never forget the impressions made upon me by the first sermon I heard him preach . . . his general appearance, the tones of his voice, and his antiquated pronunciation of words, were little calculated to awaken in me any lofty expectations of his rhetorical powers. In person, and voice, and manner, he was peculiar. If you never saw him, imagine a tall and exceedingly lean man, of a sallow (almost cadaverous) complexion; with as little of the Chesterfield in his gait or manners as you can well conceive; speaking with a harsh grating voice, and, notwithstanding his excellent education and powerful intellect, retaining many of the inaccuracies of pronunciation of his earlier years, and you will have a tolerably correct conception of the man. Although I had heard him spoken of as an eloquent preacher, I had made up my mind that it was a vulgar error. When he began the services, my attention was soon powerfully arrested . . .*

*. . . In respect to his faith and his practice, he was a thorough-going, old-fashioned Presbyterian. Some, at the present day, would call him ultra. Time and experience will attest whether his rigid adherence to the time-honoured usages of his denomination was an error or not. "Non nostrum, inter vos, tantas componere lites." He has been censured by some because he did not encourage the*

*establishment of a Sunday School in his church. This censure would
perhaps be withdrawn, if his reasons were more generally known.
His was a very large country congregation, covering more than ten
miles square, in which it would have been exceedingly difficult, if
not impossible, to assemble any considerable portion of the children
for instruction. The population, too, within his bounds, was almost
entirely Presbyterian, and the youth very generally received faithful
parental instruction at home. In addition to these facts, the Doctor,
during the warm season, —from May to October, —instructed Bible
classes, embracing all the young, and many of the aged, of his
congregation, every Sabbath, before the morning service . . .*

*. . . He has been blamed too for his supposed opposition to what
are, in common panance, termed "revivals" and "revival
preaching." To some extent this objection is unjust, because
founded on a misconception of his real views. The intimate and
cordial friendship with which the Doctor honoured me throughout
our long acquaintance to the close of his life, enables me, I think, to
present his opinions on this subject, as they were entertained by
himself. He believed that the faithful preaching of the sublime truths
of the Gospel, with the forcible presentation of its motives and
sanctions, was the only instrumentality that was either requisite or
proper for the conversion of sinners; —that urging upon the
impenitent any considerations or motives, not expressly set forth in
the Word of God, or fairly deducible from it, was (to use a legal
phrase)" travelling out of the record," and therefore improper. He
was, therefore, most decidedly opposed to what he was in the habit of
calling "mechanical means" to get up an excitement at religious
meetings; and he probably distrusted the genuineness of
conversions, where such means were used, and followed by what he
deemed their natural result, —mere animal excitement. But it is not
true that he was opposed to revivals . . .*

*. . . I have thus, my dear Sir, given you a very imperfect sketch of
the late Dr. Barr. I hope you will excuse the remarks on the subject*

*of his opinions, which do not probably come within the scope of what
you expected from me. I found it impossible to avoid those matters
in giving you my "impressions of his character," —particularly as
many of his friends in the South think that those opinions justly
derogate from his character. I confess freely that I am not one of
those who so think. In my estimation, he was a great and good
man, —not without defects, —for who is without them? —but in all
that constitutes the character of a Christian preacher, excelled by
few. I parted with him on my removal to Alabama in 1835, with
much regret; and except once, never saw him again. He lingered
and suffered a few more years, and then died, as it was believed, "the
death of the righteous." His wife is my near relative, and my
partialities may have caused me to appreciate his talents and worth
too highly. I believe, however, that the concurrent opinions of all his
intelligent acquaintances will substantially sustain mine.*[4]

Rev. Barr's prominence as a Christian minister, who was revered
by his Abbeville community and beyond, led me to question how
enslaved African Americans viewed Christianity. Consequently, I
learned that after African captives were subjugated into the inhumane
institution of chattel slavery, Christianity was hesitantly accepted by
most of them than denied. Many slaves ultimately fused the vestiges
of African traditional religions into Christian practices to maintain
some semblance of home. Ingeniously, they captured what they
needed to form their own religious foundation, thereby forming an
"invisible institution." In African traditional religions, which have
been largely misunderstood by the Western world, the African
ancestors of African Americans carried a belief in one Supreme God.
They engaged in daily interaction with divinities that were regarded as
God's intermediaries and assistants. They also possessed a profound
respect for nature.[5] The ancestors also placed high value on spiritual
communalism, in which a strong sense of belonging together prevailed.

The cleverly-crafted plan of converting Africans to Christianity began in earnest during the religious revival known as the Great Awakening of the 1730s, escalating in the late eighteenth century. As part of the revival movement, white ministers and slave-owners aimed to save the "poor black heathens" from the ways of the "dark continent" by showing them their perceived way to salvation. Many began to require some of their slaves to attend their churches, permitting them to only sit in the back or in the balconies, away from the white congregation. Periodically, slave-owners would arrange separate evening services that were held under the watchful eyes of slave-owners who instructed ministers to tailor their sermons to benefit the slave-holders. They used religion and the Bible to alter the minds of slaves to suit their own purposes. In *Incidents in the Life of a Slave Girl*, Harriet Jacobs recounted the following delivered by a white minister:

> . . . Although your masters may not find you out, God sees
> you; and will punish you. You must forsake your sinful
> ways, and be faithful servants. Obey your old master and
> your young master – your old mistress and your young
> mistress. If you disobey your earthly master, you offend your
> heavenly Master. You must obey God's commandments.
> When you go from here, don't stop at the corners of the
> streets to talk, but go directly home, and let your master and
> mistress see that you have come.[6]

Fortunately, for research purposes only, my ancestors were documented in the Session book of the Upper Long Cane Church as slave members, who were noted as "Coloured Members." The Session book of the church further documented their existence and enabled me to glean some aspects of their lives during slavery. As John had indicated, the surviving Session book covered the time period 1852 to 1869 and starts with a list of white communicants, followed by a "List of Coloured persons Members of Upper Long Cane Church August 1852 and continued with additions made after that date." The church minutes for that time period indicated that William Barr Jr. migrated to Pontotoc County, Mississippi with Fanny, Isabella, Marinda, Sawney, and Edmond shortly before March 20, 1859. All of them, except Sawney, had been the legal property of his mother Rebecca.

Additionally, the minutes revealed that Margaret Barr Cater took Sina and her husband Sam to Spartanburg, South Carolina shortly before February 26, 1860. Margaret's husband, Rev. Edwin Cater, was a Presbyterian minister who, after residing in Spartanburg for eight months, later moved with Margaret and his children to Somerville, Tennessee.[7] Sam, Sina, and their children were then transported there in the fall of 1860. Taking the Williamson surname, they later moved to Lafayette County, Mississippi during the 1870s and lived near Sina's baby sister, Susie.

On Sunday, March 20, 1859, the following church minutes were recorded:

> The moderator presented the application of the following
> persons for Letters of Dismission from this church to join Zion
> Church in Mississippi, viz, Mr. William Barr and his servants
> to wit, **Fanny, Isabella, Marinda, Sawney,** and **Edmond**. On
> motion ordered that certificates in the usual form be granted
> to them. . .

On Sunday, February 26, 1860, the following minutes were recorded:

> The clerk informed the Session that the following persons
> made application for letters of Dismission, viz, Mrs. Nancy
> Jane Bowie to join Presbyterian Church at Spartanburg; Mrs.
> Margaret R. Cater (formerly Miss Barr) to join same church . . .

**Sam** & **Sina**, servants of Mrs. Cater to join church at
Spartanburg C. H.

Incredibly, the minutes taken on Saturday, October 13, 1860
confirmed the existence of Jacob, the noted father of Sue's son, Rev.
Jacob C. Beckley. The minutes suggested that Jacob and Sue were in all
probability a slave couple who William Barr had also transported to
Pontotoc County, Mississippi, along with their children, likely during
the same time as the others. However, their letter of dismission from
the church was requested at a later date by Lemuel Reid. The church
secretary recorded the following:

> ... The clerk also stated that he had been requested by Mr.
> Lemuel Reid to present the application of **Jacob & Sue**
> servants of Wm. Barr for a Dismission from this church to join
> Harmony Church, Mississippi. Ordered that the application
> be granted and that the clerk do furnish the proper certificate
> of Dismission.

Interestingly, more evidence also indicated the paternity of Sue's
children. Since her children took the Beckley surname and were noted
as mulattoes in the 1850 slave schedule and the 1880 census,
presumably Jacob was the father of all of her children. On June 30,
1860, the census-taker counted Fanny, Jacob, Sue and most of her
children, and Isabella, Marinda, Sawney, and an unidentified female in
the Pontotoc County slave schedule as William Barr's slaves (see table
7.1). William's fifty-two-year-old mulatto male slave in 1860 was
unquestionably Jacob, who chose to take the Beckley surname after
slavery instead of Barr. Apparently, the presumably lighter
complexion of Sue's children, obviously inherited from Jacob, caused
the 1850 and 1880 census-takers to erroneously note them as mulattoes.

Even more of a genealogical treasure, a list of "Coloured
Members" was recorded in the Session book. From 1854 to 1858, my

family was listed with accompanying remarks written next to their entry during different phases of their membership. For most of them, a date when they professed their faith and were received as members was recorded. Some of them had been baptized during that time period, and their dates of baptism were also recorded. Providing further evidence that Sue and Jacob, who was recorded as being sold to William after 1852, was a couple, the third and fourth entries contained the following:

**Jacob**, servant of John W. Lesly; sold to Wm. Barr; dismissed
    13 October 1860 to join Harmony Church, Mississippi
**Sue**, servant of Mrs. R. Barr; dismissed 13 October 1860 to join
    Harmony Church, Mississippi

The following other entries for the Barr slaves were recorded in the Session book. Presumably, Jacob, Sue, Glasgow, and Sawney were originally enrolled in a previous Session book that is no longer in existence; therefore, their date of membership and baptism is not known, although it occurred before 1852:

**Glasgow**, servant of Mrs. R. Barr [no remarks]
**Sawney**, servant of Mrs. R. Barr; dismissed 20 Mar. 1859 to
    join Zion Church, Mississippi
**Fanny**, servant of Mrs. R. Barr; baptized and received 22 Oct.
    1854 on examination; dismissed 20 Mar. 1859 to join Zion
    Church, Mississippi
**Marinda**, servant of Mrs. R. Barr; baptized and received 22
    Oct. 1854 on examination; dismissed 20 Mar. 1859 to join
    Zion Church, Mississippi
**Sina**, servant of Mrs. R. Barr; baptized and received 22 Oct.
    1854 on examination; dismissed 26 Feb. 1860 to join
    Church at Spartanburg

**Sam**, servant of D. Wardlaw; received 7 April 1855 on
examination; dismissed to join Church at Spartanburg 26
Feb. 1860; sold to Mrs. M. R. (Barr) Cater

**Bella**, servant of Mrs. R. Barr; baptized and received 8 April
1855 on examination; dismissed 20 Mar. 1859 to join Zion
Church, Mississippi

**Pleasant**, servant of Wm Barr; received 17 May 1856 on
examination [no remarks]

**Edmund**, servant of Wm. Barr; received 28 Mar. 1858 on
examination; dismissed 20 Mar. 1859 to join Zion Church,
Mississippi

A list of baptisms recorded in the Session book further identified
Jacob and Sue as a couple. The following baptisms of two of their
children were recorded:

**Joseph** coloured, infant; Parents, **Jacob & Sue**; baptized 21
August 1852

**Susan Ebony**, infant of **Jacob**, servant of Barr, & **Sue**, servant
of Barr; baptized 20 Sept. 1857

Unfortunately, Grandpa Bill Reed was not recorded in the Session
book for that time period. His baptism, if it had occurred, may have
been recorded in an earlier church book that is now lost forever.
However, the following slaves of Lemuel Reid were noted as members:

**Israel**, servant of Lemuel Reid; received 16 Oct. 1852 on
examination; died early in 1867

**Abram**, servant of Lemuel Reid; baptized and received 16
Sept. 1854 on examination [no remarks]

**Leah**, servant of Lemuel Reid; baptized and received 22 Oct.
1854 on examination [no remarks]

**Lewis**, servant of Lemuel Reid; baptized and received 20 Oct. 1855 on examination; removed to Mississippi

During their membership, Glasgow and his brother-in-law, Jacob, held leadership roles among the enslaved members at Upper Long Cane Church. Fascinatingly, *Keeping the Faith: A History of the Upper Long Cane Presbyterian Church* disclosed that they were two of six enslaved members of the church who were appointed leaders of the "colored members of the congregation" in September 1858. They were noted as being "servants of William Barr." The other four men were Dave, a servant of J. Fraser Livingstone, London, a servant of T. C. Perrin, John, a servant of Rev. J. A. Hoyt, and Shadrack, a servant of William Lesley. Their duties included visiting the sick, conducting prayer meetings "so far as sanctioned by the laws of the land," and ensuring proper decorum among the enslaved members in church and elsewhere.[8]

As a result of their close affiliations with Upper Long Cane Church, religion inevitably became an integral part of some of the Barr slaves' lives after slavery. Pleasant Barr would help to establish and build the St. Paul United Methodist Church in Ripley, Mississippi, just five years after slavery. Jacob and Sue's son, Rev. Jacob C. Beckley, would minister a church in Holly Springs, Mississippi. Glasgow Barr and his wife Rose remained members of Upper Long Cane Church after slavery. They were listed on a roster of "colored members" in August 1878.

What was it like for Fanny, Glasgow, Pleasant, Sue, Isabella, Sawney, and the rest of them to attend the same church as their enslavers? What were their spiritual experiences in a church whose religious leader and members indisputably believed and invested in their enslavement? Were they forced to attend or was their attendance on a voluntary basis? What type of sermons did the minister preach specifically to them? How did they feel about attending the special services for the "coloured members" at Upper Long Cane? Rev.

Thomas A. Hoyt, who served as pastor from 1855 to 1859, held services on every other Sunday for the enslaved members.[9] While viewing the names of the 159 enslaved members who were recorded in the church's Session book, these questions and more inundated my mind.

Over time, the Barr slaves, like most enslaved African Americans, embraced Christianity; they were empowered by the Biblical messages of spiritual equality of all humans and were comforted by the Biblical themes of deliverance. Particularly, many slaves identified with the Old Testament story of the Hebrews being led by Moses out of the land of bondage in Egypt to the Promised Land. They became attached to the story of Daniel being delivered from the lion's den, from which they interpreted that God freed men from their difficult situations. These passages and others constantly gave them renewed hope for freedom, becoming a strong foundation for dealing with the many trials and tribulations slavery forced upon them in their daily lives. Although many white ministers twisted Biblical passages to suit their whims and to justify their inhumane actions, many slaves did not take their words to heart. Unable to read the Bible for themselves and being very skeptical of white preachers' interpretation, most slaves learned the message of the Christian gospel and translated it into songs in terms of their own experience.[10]

There is probably no documentation that tells of my ancestors' personal experiences at Upper Long Cane Church; however, insight was gained from the Works Progress Administration slave narratives in which former slaves described their affiliation and experiences in white churches during slavery. Hannah Austin of Ross, Georgia conveyed, "We did not have churches of our own but were allowed to attend the white churches in the afternoon. The white families attended in the forenoon. We seldom heard a true religious sermon; but were constantly preached the doctrine of obedience to our masters and mistresses. We were required to attend church every Sunday."[11]

Although many voluntarily or involuntarily attended, a number of them felt repressed in their enslavers' church. Mingo White of

Alabama expressed, "Us didn' have no whar to go 'cep' church an' we didn' git no pleasure outten it 'case we warn't 'lowed to talk from de time we lef' home 'til us got back."[12]  Equating her experience to the treatment of animals, Anna Morgan of South Carolina recounted, "Now some of 'em went to de white folks church; but dey couldn't do nuthin' – jes sit dere. Dey could sing, an' take de sacrement; but didn't have no voice – jes like animals!"[13] Similarly, Mary Ella Grandberry of Alabama expressed, "On Sundays us jes' laid 'roun' 'mos' all day. Us didn't git no pleasure outten goin' to church, 'caze we warn't 'lowed to say nothin'."[14]  This inhibition was also felt by Minerva Grubbs of Mississippi who explained, "You see, de white folks dont git in de spirit, dey don't shout, pray, hun, and sing all through de services lak us do. Dey dont believe in a heap o' things us niggers knows 'bout.[15]

For people of African descent, spiritual worship summoned a more expressive emotion than in white societies.  Africans freely incorporated shouts, yells, and moans into their style of worship and in their singing – sounds and expressions that many whites felt were unacceptable and uncivilized because of their stereotypical notions regarding Africa and its people.  The spiritual life of Africans included joyful songs, dances, and heart-felt prayers with hand-clapping, foot stomping, and call-and-response, which distinctly marked the worship services of most African Americans.  When forced to deviate from their cultural norm, the experiences were understandably displeasing, as Sarah Fitzpatrick of Alabama indicated, "Niggers' commence'ta wanna go to church by de'selves . . . niggers' lack'ta shout a whole lot an' wid de white folks al' round 'em, dey couldn't shout jes' lack dey want to."[16]

As I emotionally digested what the church records had revealed, the floodgates of information regarding the history of the Barr slaves remained ajar. *"When it rains, it pours"* is an idiom that means that once something happens after a long break, it happens in large amounts. Correspondingly, for over two years, I had wondered about the whereabouts of the family members from whom Grandpa Bill Reed and his father, Pleasant, had been forever separated. After this prolonged time of patience and wonderment, the events of my family history during slavery unfolded through a series of historical discoveries from a number of valuable records. Much more was forthcoming.

*This is an artistic description of a slave preaching to a congregation of slaves in a "rude chapel erected for the slaves" on a cotton plantation near Port Royal, South Carolina. Instead of attending the enslaver's church, many slaves on large plantations attended slave churches there on the plantation.*

*Source: "The Atlantic Slave Trade and Slave Life in the Americas: A Visual Record," (http://hitchcock.itc.virginia.edu/Slavery/index.php), The Illustrated London News (Dec. 5, 1863), vol. 43, p. 561.*

The first page of the "List of Coloured persons Members of Upper Long Cane Church August 1852 and continued with additions made after that date" from the Session book of the Upper Long Cane Presbyterian Church, Abbeville South Carolina. Pleasant Barr's sister, Sue, and her husband, Jacob, are the third and fourth entries.

# Chapter 9

## "The negroes are to be divided."

he rain of information continued pouring and the floodgates widened two months after receiving the church records; so much so, that I needed a larger umbrella. I received an e-mail from a Reid descendant, Bob Thompson, who was an avid genealogist and also a great-great-grandson of Rebecca Barr's sister, Margery Reid Miller. We had been communicating online periodically about the Reid and Barr families of Abbeville County. Bob was transcribing old Reid and Miller family letters. He conveyed, "I have just transcribed a letter dated February 6, 1849 from Rebecca Barr in Abbeville, to her sister, Margery Miller, in Pontotoc . . . I thought a reference to Sue would be of interest to you.[1]

Indeed, it was of great interest. Several days later, a copy of the letter arrived in the mail from Bob. It was an eye-opener. Rebecca's letter, that she asked her sister to discard after reading it, exposed her plans to divide the slaves. She desired that some of them be taken to Mississippi, while others remain there in Abbeville. However, she desired to keep Sue and her children together. Her fondness of Sue

A portion of the first page of Rebecca Reid Barr's letter to her sister, dated February 6, 1849, which disclosed her plans to divide the family slaves. Courtesy of Bob Thompson

was evident, as it implied that Sue was probably her house servant who had close interactions with her. In 1849, Rebecca wrote this secretive letter to Margery:

Dear Sister,

I received your letter several weeks ago. It affords me a great deal of pleasure to hear from you. I feel the loss of you now more than I ever did. Almost all my good neighbors have died and moved away. Nancy J. Bowie is the only near neighbour that visits me. Betsey Ann comes to see me as often as she can. She is very kind to me. Mrs. David Lesley &

several of the Ladys in the village visit me occasionly. I am not with out friends and the common comforts of life. But I can not feel altogether satisfied to be so far from my older sons. If we can sell our plantation to advantage we will move to Miss. I cannot expect to live long enough to be a comfortably fix there as here but I think my children can do better there, **and at my Death the negroes are to be divided. Some will go to Miss. and some here and I cannot bear the idea of sepperating Sue and her children.** She has nine children—seven sons & two daughters. They are very smart and promising in every respect. She is an uncommon good negro—honest and Faithful and very kind to me.

You will be surprised to hear that cousin Betsey Baskin is in this country. She lives in Missourria and was on a visit to her children in Virginia. Her Brother James went to se her and brought her home with him. She will stay until spring. Her Brother John came to se her. He came to se me. He is quit fleshy and looks very much like Mother. Betsey has not been to se me yet but promised to come. She is the only daughter living. Mrs. Lesley is still living and better than she has been in a long time. She cannot walk much. Mrs. Gordens health is so bad she cannot go to church or any whare els.

Rose Ann Gilmore is pretty well. Eliza has ten sons living. I heard from Dr. Norwoods a few days ago. They ware all well. Fanny and Louisa staid with us four weeks this winter. They are nearly grown. Lu is beautiful. Jane is not in a family way. Her health is very good now. I am glad to hear Jude is so useful in her old days. Lucy is still living but frail. She is still very useful to her master. Her daughter Jude has left all her children but one and gone with one of the meanest of husbands to Florida. My rheumatism is rather better. I do not suffer so much as I did last winter but I have no hopes of ever walking. My health is very good and a sew a great deal and do every thing that I can do sitting. I am no charge yet. I hear from John Henry frequently. He is doing well. I hope you will come to se us. I think it would be of service to Sarah to come too. I have just heard the Jane Baird is at James Kyle's I suppose they are out of a home. I don't think they will ever stay long in one place. When you see her write me and let me know all about them. I have written you all that will interest you. Dont let anyone see my letter. I write with a bad pen and when I write a few lines my hand becomes crampt and I write in pain.

Your affectionate Sister,
Rebecca Barr[2]

Approximately ten years later, Rebecca Barr's wish of dividing the rest of the slaves was fulfilled. This was a detrimental act that annihilated the solid family unit that Lewis and Fanny had procreated on the Barr farm. This division occurred nearly four years before her death in January 1863. Her requests were executed at the emotional pain and suffering of my ancestors who never saw each other again. This was heart-breaking.

For nearly a decade after her letter, while Lewis, Fanny, Glasgow, Pleasant, Sue, Isabella, and the rest labored on the Barr farm, they were probably unaware that they would be separated from each other in the near future. Being approximately three years old, Grandpa Bill Reed was too young to comprehend the impending doomsday. Perhaps, they had heard that a move to Mississippi was inevitable, thinking and hoping that they would all be transported there together. This likely did not ring a good sound in Fanny's ears, who had already endured a permanent move to unknown territory. She had been brought to South Carolina from somewhere in Virginia, possibly as a young girl who was separated from her own family. Prior to Rebecca's death, but still in accordance with her wishes, the following four upsetting events in my family history occurred:

1. By the spring of 1859, William Barr Jr. had transported most of them to Pontotoc County, Mississippi. Fanny's daughter Sue and her children were kept together, as Rebecca had desired, and taken to Mississippi.
2. Shortly before their exodus to Mississippi, Fanny's son, Pleasant, was sold to James Giles, who took him to Ripley, Mississippi, never to see Grandpa Bill again.
3. Grandpa Bill and most likely his younger sister, Mary, were sold to her nephew, Lemuel Reid, and remained there in Abbeville until slavery ended.
4. Fanny's son, Glasgow, was also left in Abbeville; quite plausibly, he remained there on the now-empty Barr farm with the elderly Rebecca up until her death since all of her children and the rest of the slaves were not on the farm.

The act of separating slave families seemed second nature to Rebecca, as deemed from her letter to Margery on December 22, 1838. As a woman who felt that honest and caring enslaved women like Sue were uncommon, she cavalierly described to her sister the selling of their sister Elizabeth "Betsey" Reid Wilson's slaves, along with the material items of her estate and the livestock that had to be sold to settle her estate. Betsey had died on the 29th of July of that year. To Rebecca, everything was just property to generate finances for her sister's children. To me, slaves were people – resilient human beings who God had created to be such and who lived in a society that enforced the status of slave upon them. They were people who greatly esteemed their families and who shed a river of tears when they were torn away from them. They were the direct ancestors of many African Americans who are totally oblivious about the dismal day in November 1838 when they were placed on the auction block.

Devastatingly, the slaves that were sold included a mother and her children. Rebecca wrote:

I received your letter by Mr. Hamilton and designed answering it immediately, but as usual I had a great deal to do, and postponed untill now. Sister Betseys property was sold the first of November. The property did not sell well. **Norman** sold for 800 and 25 dollars. **Alfred** for 836. **Letty and child** for 450. James Lesly bought **Carry** for 500, and the **2 youngest children** for 280 dolers. Jane got **Alice** for 200. She had the scrofula in her neck which made her sell low, but they opened it when small and it is now well. The cattle and hogs sold well, but Yankee sold for 13 dollars and old Fan for one doller. After feeding away a great deal of corn to them which sold near a doller per bushel they ware very fat. A great many things in the house were sacrificed & James Lesley told me he would sell Elizas bed, if I would bye it. I promised to do so. I had to pay 20 cnts per pound, the other beds sold at 31 and 25 cnts, but I do not regrett paying so much. It is a good bed. The Idea of its being Elizas makes me partial to it. James Lesley acted very honorably. No person bid against him for the negroes and he bid several times upon his own bid. He has acted like a Father and brother both to these poor orphans. I hope he will be rewarded for his kindness. Leroy Wilson bought **Norman** and David Lesley bid **Alfred** off, but he was unwiling to live with him or go to James Kyle and said he wanted to go to Harvey Wilson & David let Harvy have him. Mrs. Martin (widow) bought **Letty**. The plantation was sold last sale day. Brother Sam bought it at 3100 dollars. The children will have more than 1000 doller a piece.[3]

As Bob Thompson continued his transcription of the Reid and Miller family letters, he informed me of other tidbits of information mentioned in them that may be of historical interest to me. I was very grateful. Indeed, another eye-opening letter was one that Rebecca wrote to Margery on February 13, 1847. She revealed in that letter the death of Lewis. He had died in September 1846. This explained why he was not counted in the 1850 slave schedule. Rebecca Barr wrote:

> . . . Lemuel Reids family has had a great deal of sickness. His negro man Abram was very low indeed some weeks ago but is recovering . . .We are now preparing for another crop. William has been railing in the yard, has cut down a great many of the trees and sowing it in blue grass, and has railed in a very large garden and built new negro houses . . . I suppose you have heard that my old Negro man Lewis is dead. He died in September. I hope he was prepared for death.[4]

Fortunately, Lewis joined the ancestors before he could witness the involuntary breakup of the family he and Fanny birthed. I pictured my ancestor's body laying on a cooling board, while his adult sons, Glasgow and Pleasant, made a wooden coffin. I pictured his wife, Fanny, and their daughter, Sue, sitting up all night guarding the body from prowling animals. I pictured them and the rest singing and praying all through the night as they prepared for a midnight burial. This was a typical practice since slaves usually had to work during the day.[5] The funeral rites were probably given days later, on a partial workday that Rebecca or William permitted so that they could properly send Lewis home to be with the ancestors. I pictured Glasgow and Pleasant digging a grave that faced the east-west, with Lewis' head facing the west and his eyes facing Africa. I pictured his grave being decorated with the last articles that he used; this was an African custom. Lewis was now free.

Photograph of the slave auction block at Green Hill Plantation, Campbell County, Virginia. Source: The Historic American Building Survey, The Library of Congress, Washington, D.C.

# Chapter 10

## The Ties That Bind

*I* have been told many times by friends and strangers that I look a lot like someone they know. In some cases, the person to whom I resemble was not from Mississippi and did not have roots in Mississippi, as far as they were aware. One time, Mom thought that a young model in a shaving cream advertisement looked so much like me that she mailed the advertisement to me with a notation saying, "Your twin." Although I begged to differ, my father and my sister agreed with Mom.

Learning how many African Americans had been torn away from their families during slavery in great numbers, I often wonder how many times I and many others have been in the presence of someone who was actually a blood family member – perhaps a descendant of a long-lost sibling of an enslaved ancestor who was taken away. Naturally, I wondered about the family members of Grandpa Bill Reed and Pleasant Barr from whom they were torn asunder. Perhaps, they have descendants who I and other Reeds have actually met but was completely oblivious of the familial connection. Perhaps, African

Americans who meet someone who resembles a member of their family may actually be a not-so-distant cousin through ties that were broken during slavery. As I pondered, I became increasingly curious about the descendants of the Barr slaves and wondered if I could ever bind those broken ties.

As I browsed through the Pontotoc County marriage records and the censuses of 1880, 1900, 1910, and 1920, I clearly saw that four of Sue's sons, Edmond, Cannon, Henry Clay, and Lewis Beckley, lived the rest of their lives in Pontotoc County, while their brother, Rev. Jacob C. Beckley, had migrated to Holly Springs, Mississippi – which was only thirty-two miles from Grandpa Bill Reed's farm. Those four brothers produced very large families. Many more relatives lived in an area of northern Mississippi where I would have never imagined that Grandpa Bill's family members were taken after he waved goodbye to them in Abbeville, South Carolina. They were less than seventy-five miles away. If one places the pin of a compass directly on Pontotoc, Mississippi on a map and draw a circle with a radius of seventy-five miles around it, the towns of Ripley, Oxford, Senatobia, and Holly Springs would be situated inside the circle. Grandpa Bill's oblivion of his close proximity to his family members will forever be mind-boggling.

Interestingly, the families of the four brothers had grown by leaps and bounds since slavery. By 1920, many of their descendants resided in the same area of Pontotoc County where William Barr Jr. had transplanted most of the Barr slaves by the spring of 1859. Lewis Beckley had even lived until 1942, five years after Grandpa Bill's death. Edmond Beckley had married twice, to Jane (maiden name unknown) and then to Jane Dillard, and fathered fourteen children. Cannon Beckley had married Lucy Black and later to Eliza Weatherall. He was the father of twenty children. Their sister, Louvenia Beckley, also remained in the area and had one daughter. Henry Clay Beckley, who had married Martha Brooks and later to Lennie Franklin, fathered fourteen children. Rev. Jacob C. Beckley married and had two daughters. Lewis Beckley had married Alberta Wells, and they had seven children.

Were there any surviving descendants of any of them? Surely, there had to be. I then began a quest to try to locate someone. Anyone. What a powerful reunion this would be – two descendants of a brother and a sister, Pleasant and Sue, who were forcibly separated during slavery. How would I be received? Would they have knowledge of the things I had uncovered over the past ten years?

Enthusiastically, I began my online quest to bind the broken ties. I had been inundated in records of dead people for so long that I was ready to enter into the land of the living. I went to the U.S. GenWeb site for Pontotoc County to see if someone was researching the Beckley surname. Indeed, someone named S. M. Rutherford listed that surname, along with other surnames, with an e-mail address. That genealogy query had been on the site for five years, since December 10, 1997. I immediately sent a message to the posted address, hoping that it was still valid. In my e-mail, I inquired if her Beckleys were white or African-American, and I explained that I was looking for the descendants of the four Beckley brothers who lived and died in Pontotoc County after slavery. Since no white Beckleys lived in Pontotoc County and the surrounding counties, I was confident that she was researching African-American Beckleys and was one of the descendants. Luckily, the e-mail was not immediately returned with an error message to indicate that the address had expired. Therefore, I was optimistic.

In the meantime, I posted a message on another online genealogy message board simply stating, "I am researching the Beckley Family of Pontotoc County, Mississippi, five brothers from South Carolina: Edmond, Cannon, Jacob, Henry, and Lewis Beckley. They arrived in Mississippi before 1860. Any info on this family will be appreciated."

After several agonizing days of waiting, I received a response from S. M. Rutherford. My heart pounded as I opened the e-mail. Excitingly, she disclosed that her name was Susie Rutherford, the great-granddaughter of Susan Beckley Thomas, for whom she was named, and Susan was the daughter of Cannon Beckley. I starred at the computer screen for a minute, frozen in thought.

"Oh my God, her name is Susie!" I shouted at the screen, realizing the significance of this first communication.

I sat there in disbelief before responding to her e-mail. The first descendant of my great-great-grandfather's sister who I found was someone who carried her name. Although Susie Rutherford claimed that she was named after her great-grandmother, her great-grandmother was named after her grandmother, Cannon's mother. Therefore, the origins of her name can actually be traced back to her great-great-great-grandmother, Sue "Barr" Beckley. Not only that, Cannon was the only one of Sue's sons whose name was clearly remembered by Cousin Ike when he recalled the stories that Grandpa Bill Reed had shared with him. And now, the first descendant of Sue who I found was Cannon's great-great-granddaughter. I continued to sit at the computer in utter disbelief.

Susie informed me in her e-mail that the brothers, including Rev. Jacob C. Beckley, were known in their family history as the Beckley Five. What a unique name that displayed family unity. She further shared that the Beckley Family holds a family reunion every year. In fact, they began the tradition of annual reunions in 1957. Subsequent reunions were held in 1958 and in 1959 and restarted in 1974. Additionally, Susie amazingly shared that she was aware of a Barr connection to the Beckley Five, but they had no luck figuring out that connection. I was thrilled and honored to disclose some facts about our family history, and how her name originally came from Cannon's mother. Susie was, indeed, overwhelmed.

Susie and I finally talked by phone several days later. In our e-mail correspondence, she had not disclosed where she was from, but I gave her my phone number because I wanted to hear her voice – to actually talk with a descendant of Sue. She called and we soon discovered that we both reside in Memphis. To add to the growing list of shocking revelations, she shared that Dr. David L. Beckley, the current and eleventh president of Rust College since 1993, is a great-great-grandson of Cannon Beckley. Rust College was Mom and Aunt Eartha's alma mater. Also, the second African-American president, Dr. Lee Marcus McCoy, whose father assisted Pleasant Barr and the board of trustees to secure land in Ripley for a church in 1870, had helped them to secure financial aid. And now, the current president is a descendant of Pleasant's sister, Sue. This was unbelievable! The ironies of history had begun to unfold. I soon called Mom to share this wonderful discovery.

I then called Cousin Leroy Frazier, who was also a Rust College alumnus and who was fascinated by the things being uncovered about Grandpa Bill Reed's history. The phone conversation with Cousin Leroy is a permanent fixture in my sound mind; he also disclosed more shocking revelations.

"Cousin Leroy, I found the whereabouts of some of Grandpa Bill's family. His father had a sister named Sue who was married to a man who became a Beckley. She and her children were taken to Pontotoc County, Mississippi along with more of Grandpa Bill's family members."

"That is amazing! I am familiar with the Beckley name," Cousin Leroy shared.

"Really? Do you know Dr. David Beckley, the president of Rust College," I asked.

"Yes, that's how I am familiar with the Beckley name. He is a colleague of mines, and we attended Rust together in the 70s," Cousin Leroy further shared.

I continued, "Well, he is our cousin. He is a descendant of one of Sue's sons named Cannon, the same Cannon listed on that Barr inventory I showed you." There was a long pause.

"Are you sure, Cousin Mel," he expressed in disbelief.

I replied excitingly, "Oh yes! I am very sure! I even looked him up on the Internet and he looks like family, too. He looks a lot like the Reeds!"

"Are you sure, Cousin Mel," Cousin Leroy asked again.

"Yes, a Beckley cousin here in Memphis told me," I conveyed.

"I do not believe this, Cousin Mel. This is amazing! Dr. Beckley and I have been colleagues for over twenty years. In fact, when we attended Rust, some people would mistake me for him and claimed that we favored each other. Cousin Mel, this is absolutely amazing!"

Again, there was silence on the phone. Cousin Leroy needed time to mentally process what he had learned.

Susie Rutherford advised me to talk with the Grand Matriarch of the Beckley Family. This is an important role bequeathed to an elder of the family, and this position had been bestowed upon a Tupelo, Mississippi resident, Sina Ella Hadley Ruff. Stunned by the fact that she too carried another family name, I soon called her but with initial hesitation. This was not coincidence that the first two of Sue's descendants, who I would communicate with, carried family names. The ancestors were sending a clear message of approval.

But, how do I explain to Sina Ella on the phone that I was a descendant of her ancestor's brother who was sold away in slavery? Would she believe me? How would she receive me? Would she think that I was a prank caller or a con artist? A day after receiving her phone number, I nervously picked up the phone and made the call – another phone conversation that has a permanent place in my sound mind.

"Hello," answered an elderly yet strong voice.

"May I speak to Mrs. Sina Ella Ruff, please," I said, still nervous.

"This is Sina Ella," she answered.

"Mrs. Ruff, my name is Melvin Collier. Your cousin, Susie Rutherford, gave me your phone number. I am calling you because I have been researching my family history for several years, and I recently discovered that I am related to the Beckley Family."

"Oh really, how?" she questioned.

"Well, Mrs. Ruff, this is going to sound strange, but my great-grandfather was named Bill Reed. He lived near Senatobia, and he had been a slave of the Barrs in South Carolina. His father was named Pleasant Barr, and I recently discovered that Pleasant had a sister who was the mother of the Beckley brothers. Her name was Sue," I explained.

"You don't say! Well, I had heard that there was a connection to the Barr name. My cousin in Memphis had done some research on the family several years ago, but she couldn't figure out how we were linked to the Barr name," she shared.

By this time, I became comfortable because she listened to me without hanging up. Also, the mention of the Barr name seemed to have given her assurance that I was not a con artist.

I continued, "Did you know that the Beckley brothers had a sister named Sina? She was their oldest sister."

"Yes, I did. My grandmother's father was Lewis Beckley, and I was always told that I was named after one of his sisters. There was another sister named Louvenia, and Cut'n Hattie Beckley was her daughter. They had some more sisters too, from what I understand."

I explained, "Yes, Sue had at least four daughters named Sina, Louvenia, Patsy, and Susie."

"We had heard about the sisters, and we tried to find out more about them, but we haven't had much luck. You know, their father was white, and I had heard that they had several white half-sisters who taught them how to read and write."

"Oh really," I said, confused by her statement.

I had positively uncovered that the father of Sue's children was named Jacob, a mulatto slave of William Barr Jr.; therefore, this piece of oral history she relayed seemed very puzzling to me. Nevertheless, I chose not to elaborate on the paternity of Sue's children during this first phone conversation. From my communication with other family historians, I had learned that tactfulness and caution have to be employed when disclosing historical findings that emphatically disprove what an elder believes to be the absolute truth. Perhaps, I will get a chance to show her my research findings in the near future.

I continued, "Well, I've never been to Pontotoc, and my family doesn't know anything about the Beckleys because my great-great-grandfather, Pleasant Barr, was sold away, and his son, my great-grandfather, Bill Reed, came to Senatobia after the Civil War from South Carolina. The Barrs had sold him to a Reid, and that's how my family became Reeds. My great-grandfather married and had a large family, and we never knew much about his roots and his family members. But, I recently learned how they had all come from the Barr farm near Abbeville, South Carolina, and how your branch of the family ended up in Pontotoc County."

Sina Ella expressed, "This is very interesting! I am glad that you called me. I'd never heard anything about being kin to a Reed Family. Did my cousin Susie tell you about the family reunions we have? I would like to meet you and see your research. I'd love for you to come to the next reunion. It's going to be in Orlando, Florida."

"I'll be happy to show you some things that I found out," I stated. She opened the door to further communication, and I was thrilled about the opportunity to show her what all had been discovered about our history that a phone conversation could not sufficiently explain.

Our wonderful conversation continued for several more minutes. She shared with me the places where the Beckley Family Reunions had been held and the massive attendance numbers of the past. She had chaired several reunions that had been held there in Tupelo, Mississippi, just ten miles east of where the Beckleys lived in Pontotoc County. During the 1970s and 1980s, the reunions had been attended by over five hundred family members – primarily the descendants of Edmond, Cannon, Henry Clay, Lewis, and Louvenia Beckley. Remarkably, the family was so large, and their reunions were so popular, that eight Beckley Family Clubs were organized in Milwaukee, Wisconsin, Memphis, Tennessee, Chicago, Illinois,

*The 1975 Beckley Family Reunion in Pontotoc County, Mississippi, the first reunion held in Mississippi. Courtesy of Sherman Price, a descendant of Cannon Beckley*

Cleveland, Ohio, Tupelo, Mississippi, Rochester, New York, St. Louis, Missouri, and Voorhees, New Jersey. A family club in Atlanta, Georgia was later formed.

To find a blood connection to a receptive family is a wonderful thing, but to find a blood connection to an enormous family who holds very large, organized reunions was, indeed, a diamond in the ruff. Meeting more cousins was definitely inevitable.

Unfortunately, I was not able to attend the 2002 reunion in Florida, and shortly afterwards, Sina Ella passed away before I could meet her. I was disappointed, but grateful, nonetheless, that we shared a beautiful conversation.

Two months later, I received an e-mail message with the heading, "Beckley Family." Ouida Howard accidentally saw my online query and responded. She later shared that she was actually trying to find their family reunion website that her cousin, Preston Beckley IV, had built to show to her co-worker. Not remembering the website address, she entered "Beckley Family" in the search engine to find it, and my

The Milwaukee Beckley Club that was formed in 1957. Picture taken in 1959. Courtesy of Sherman Price

post came up in the search results. She clicked on it, read it, and took time to respond to it.

She expressed, "This is my family! I am a descendant of Clay Beckley. I may have information for you."

Thrilled by her message, I explained my connection to the Beckley Family. We continued corresponding via e-mail, sharing pictures of each other as if we were two long-lost siblings who had never met. We were not siblings, but we were cousins who descended from the same ancestors, Lewis and Fanny Barr.

She further shared exactly how she was Henry Clay Beckley's great-great-granddaughter. Her mother, Everjean Brame Cobb, was the daughter of Martha Beckley Brame, who was the daughter of Lemuel "Lem" Beckley, who was the son of Henry Clay.

"Ouida's great-grandfather was named Lemuel!" I shouted.

Undoubtedly, Henry Clay Beckley had named one of his sons after Lemuel Reid. I was communicating with a descendant of the man who took care of Isabella Barr after she had been separated from her own family. Not only that, Ouida's great-grandfather was named after the man to whom Grandpa Bill had been sold. More ironies of history were unfolding. This revelation left me temporarily speechless.

Ouida soon scanned and e-mailed me a copy of the Beckley family history that had been printed in their reunion books for several decades. I opened the e-mail with anticipation. Would it confirm some of the facts I had uncovered. Would it acknowledge their link to the Barr name? Perhaps, they had knowledge of my ancestor, Pleasant. Upon reading the history, my excitement quickly turned to utter confusion. The author of the history was not given, but it began as such:

> Sometime before the end of the Civil War, the oldest son of nine black children born to a slave owner by the name of Beckley killed a night rider defending his family. In order to protect his son, Beckley purchased a plantation in Barrtown, Mississippi (which later was to become known as College Hill) and moved the five brothers, Cannon, Edmond, Jacob, Clay, and Lewis; four sisters, Sina, Susie, Lucinda, and Patsy, along with their mother to Mississippi.
>
> Mississippi profited by the presence of the Beckley family who had been taught to read and write by two white half sisters, even though it was against the law to teach slaves. The brothers were skilled craftsmen. Lewis, the youngest, could also graft fruit trees. Clay was a blacksmith and dentist. Cannon and Edmond were known as big time farmers after the War. Jacob was a minister. He and Lewis purchased and donated land, which was used to find the first CME church and school in College Hill. Susie and Sina were teachers in the school. Jacob later moved to Holly Springs, Mississippi, where he was to become the presiding elder of the local C.M.E. District . . .

I immediately noticed several things that conflicted with the information I had uncovered, and I knew to be factual. There had obviously been several myths that had been passed down in the family for decades. How was I going to approach the family with genealogical information that dispelled the stories they had believed for so long? Other genealogists on AfriGeneas.com advised me to present what I had uncovered, with accompanying documentation, and "let the chips fall where they may." If the factual information is receptive, that would be great. If not, there was not anything that I could have done. I was strongly advised not to play the "convincing game." If information is presented cautiously and effectively, with documented facts, over time the unreceptive ones may come around after digesting the facts. On the other hand, as many genealogists had experienced, there will be some people, especially elders, who will never accept the documented findings over the sensationalized stories. That was beyond my control.

The myths that could be proven as false included:

**Myth 1: The slave-owner of the Beckley family was a Beckley who brought them and their mother to Mississippi.**

Truth: William Barr Jr. was the last slave-owner of the Beckley brothers, their mother Sue, and three of their four sisters, who transported them, along with their grandmother Fanny and others, to Pontotoc County, Mississippi by the spring of 1859.

**Myth 2: The Beckley slave-owner was their father.**

Truth: The father of the Beckley children was not the slave-owner. Sue's husband was named Jacob, a mulatto, who either became Jacob Beckley after the Civil War or he may have clandestinely carried the Beckley name during slavery. William Barr Jr. had purchased Jacob from John W. Lesley and transported him to Mississippi with the rest of the Barr slaves. There is a preponderance of evidence that he was the father of all of Sue's children.

**Myth 3: The mother of the Beckley children had a total of nine children.**

Truth: Sue was the mother of the following twelve children: Sina, John, Luther, Edmond, Cannon, Louvenia, Henry Clay, Jacob, Lewis, Joseph, Patsy, and Susie. Nine of them were born by February 1849, as Rebecca Barr indicated in her letter, and the remaining children were born after 1849. The slave schedules indicate that Sue may have had at least two more children who probably died at a young age.

**Myth 4: The Beckley brothers' sisters, Susie and Sina, were teachers at the College Hill School in Pontotoc County, Mississippi.**

Truth: Susie, Sina, as well as Patsy, resided in Lafayette County, Mississippi. The census-taker reported that they were washerwomen.

**Myth 5: The Beckley children had been taught to read and write by two white half-sisters.**

Truth: The children of Sue did not have any white half-sisters because their father was not white but a mulatto, probably the son of a white man and a slave mother. However, I could not help but wonder if this story had some grain of truth. Perhaps, it was actually about their father, who probably had white half-siblings.

In researching the histories of many African-American families, many people have been and will be confronted with miscegenation, a term derived from the Latin words *miscere*, which means to mix, and *genus*, which means race. The birth of many mulatto children throughout slavery was the result of the sexual exploitation of many enslaved girls and women by white slave-owners, overseers, or other men of the community. In some instances, like that of President Thomas Jefferson and his mulatto slave and half-sister-in-law, Sally

Hemings, these sexual relations were not always involuntary occurrences. Some of the relationships between white men and enslaved females contained mutual admiration, and in some cases, love. As uncovered in the PBS documentary, *African-American Lives 2*, award-winning actor Morgan Freeman's great-great-grandmother, Celia Johnson, bore several children by a white man, Alfred Carr, who worked on the plantation where she was enslaved. Census records show that Alfred, Celia, and their children lived together in one household after slavery. Laws of the land prevented them from marrying. Interestingly, the graves of Alfred and Celia were found side by side on the same plantation. Most mulatto children from these types of unions were largely unacknowledged by many of their white family members.

Because Jacob Beckley was counted as a mulatto in the 1860 slave schedule, and the color of Sue's children was also noted as mulatto in the 1850 slave schedule and the 1880 census, one can plausibly assert that all, some, or most of Sue's children may have been light-complexioned. Therefore, I understood why the family may have interpreted that the father of Sue's children was a nameless white Beckley who was proudly acknowledged in their family history. Perhaps, Jacob was a white-looking mulatto slave who could have easily passed as a full-blooded European.

A common and often erroneous presumption among many African Americans is that if the father of an enslaved ancestor was white, the father was the slave-owner who carried the same surname. In many cases, that is false. Utilizing DNA technology, some researchers have been able to prove that their mulatto ancestor was not fathered by the last enslaver. In the PBS series, *African-American Lives*, Harvard professor Dr. Henry Louis Gates learned through DNA that an Irishman named Samuel Brady, who was the last enslaver and believed to be the father of his great-great-grandmother Jane Gates' children, could not have fathered them. Nevertheless, when the DNA results were revealed to his aunt Helen, she uttered, "I've been a Brady eighty-nine years, and I am still a Brady, no matter what that test says."

During my teenage years, my fair-skinned paternal grandmother, with whom I had a very close relationship, would often speak of her mother and her mother's siblings, the Kennedys of Leake County, Mississippi, who were "mighty near white." They were the children of a mulatto slave mother and an unidentified white man. Family lore claims that they could have easily passed as Europeans, which was comprehensible since they were only one-fourth Black. However, society's "one drop" rule deemed them as Black. When my great-grandmother and her sisters traveled to town, Carthage, Mississippi, they had to wear a bandana on their heads so that they would not be mistaken for white women. As a child growing up in a society where most African Americans did not esteem their African heritage, having white ancestry, or even Native American ancestry, was a badge of honor. Admittedly, I recall being proud to know that I was not of pure African descent – anything but Black.

At the time, I did not know that ignorance of my history was the foundation of this destructive pride. I was not taught about the African contributions to world civilization. I was not taught that Africans built the pyramids of Egypt. I was not taught about Ghana, Mali, Songhai, and the other great kingdoms of Africa. I was not taught about the technologies from the African people of ancient Kemet, like the invention of the calendar, paper, and even medicine, in which Europeans had claimed as their own creations. Not once did any of my school books mention that Africans were the first philosophers, mathematicians, artists, musicians, architects, and builders. I had grown up in Mississippi, a state with a very racist past and where many people shied away from honoring their Africanity. Why? Because the images we saw of Africa from Hollywood and television were predominantly of half-naked African people in jungles wearing grass skirts. I did not know that this strategically planned imagery was the result of racism. As I began to read more about Africa in college and in graduate school, I started to feel a deeper connection to the continent and its people.

When Africans were captured and placed on slave ships to be transported to the Americas, they were not ashamed of who they were, even before the transatlantic slave trade. Feeling ashamed was incomprehensible. Although they were tightly shackled in chains and gruesomely packed together in the belly of slave ships, they did not consider themselves inferior to anyone. They were not a self-hating people as they endured the horrific, lengthy voyages across the Atlantic Ocean. They saw their black skin as beautiful, and they did not consider their hair to be "bad" or "nappy." In fact, the term "nappy" was not even in their vocabulary. Having "good hair" was something unheard of; hair was just hair. They were proud of who they were.

So, when did things start to change? How did we go from being a proud people of African descent to a people who lacked the desire to recognize our rich African heritage? How did we get transformed into a self-hating people? In contrast, author Dr. Kenneth L. Waters asserts that gang violence and drive-by shootings, drug trafficking and drug-use, black-on-black crime, and victimizations are all symptoms of a people who have been taught and who believe that nothing good has come out of Africa.[1]

American slavery has undeniably done a lot of irrevocable damage to past and present people of African descent in America. This "peculiar institution" was carefully orchestrated to obliterate the identities of our African forbears. They had African names before they were brought to America, but they were systematically stripped of those names. In its attempt to further remove the vestiges of Africa from African captives and their offspring, America told African Americans that their ancestors did not contribute anything to world civilization. Western societal ideologies falsely characterized Africa as an uncivilized continent and African people as savages. America systematically failed to record great and truthful details concerning

African people's legacy in this country and in the world. This deliberate failure continued throughout the centuries that slavery prevailed and many years afterwards.

Additionally, America's slave codes also prohibited Africans from gathering with other Africans, especially of similar ethnic backgrounds, outlawed many rituals connected with African religious practices, including dancing and the use of drums, and in many places, banned African languages.[2] These stringently enforced codes remained largely unaltered until 1865, when slavery ended. Even more demoralizing, the institution of chattel slavery often dismantled enslaved family structures that were formed on plantations and farms throughout the South. Like in Grandpa Bill Reed's history, a number of enslaved children were sold or transferred to other owners at young ages, forever separating them from parents and grandparents who could have passed on some knowledge of their African ancestral backgrounds. Consequently, this created a significant gap between African Americans and their Africanity – a psychological gap that enabled this seed of Black inferiority, which was not planted by people of African descent, to take root and grow.

How would the Beckleys take a person from out of nowhere telling them that some things in their written history are false? How would the family react to the research findings that disclose that Jacob, the father of Sue's children, was a slave and not a white Beckley? How would they feel to see that Sue's children could not have possibly had any white half-siblings to teach them to read and write? Would they have the same type of reaction as Dr. Gates's aunt? What would that do to their identity? I was very worried.

Perhaps, including information linking the Beckley surname to the white Bickley Family who had resided in Abbeville County, South Carolina may soothe the blow. My own curiosity led me to find that a man named Lieutenant John Bickley, who was born circa 1737 in Louisa County, Virginia, had died in 1801 in Abbeville District. He and his family had moved to Abbeville circa 1799. The 1800 Abbeville

District census taker recorded their surname as "Beckley." However, in the 1810 and later censuses, the name is "Bickley." Therefore, there were definite leads to the origins of the Beckley surname and to possibly the reason why Jacob, who was born around 1808, may have chosen this surname instead of either Barr or Lesley. I had been down this road before when revealing my research findings that did not corroborate with certain aspects of the oral history. That journey had not been entirely pleasant. Nevertheless, I felt that Grandpa Bill Reed would want me to continue connecting with the descendants of family members, from whom he was separated, and deal with any potential backlash that may come from presenting the facts.

Fortunately, word had spread among more family members about my research and the Beckleys' blood connection to Grandpa Bill Reed and Pleasant Barr. I received an e-mail from another Beckley cousin, Vikki Jenkins, who was excited about the things I had uncovered. At the same time, I learned that others were not enthused but skeptical. However, Vikki was not a skeptic. In her e-mail, she expressed, "I have some information that I want you to see regarding our connection to the Barrs."

Vikki soon faxed to me documents dated March and April 1977 from a genealogist that was hired by Edmond Beckley's granddaughter, Florence Bolden. Florence solicited the genealogical services of Hazel Neat of Pontotoc, Mississippi to document the family history just two months after the airing of *Roots*. Like the television mini-series had done for so many other African Americans, *Roots* had sparked Florence's desire to try to unearth her family history.

Interestingly, the information that had been uncovered had also dispelled some of the long-time oral history accounts that were continually being passed down. Vikki was, indeed, a jewel. We quickly exchanged phone numbers, which was the beginning of a beautiful friendship between two cousins who knew nothing of each other before this time. Perhaps, the information that she possessed, combined with my research findings, would help to erase the skepticism.

Astonishingly, the faxes from Vikki contained the correspondences between Florence and Hazel about her genealogical findings. Hazel had shared her discoveries from the 1880 Pontotoc County census that show the Beckleys' connection to Fanny Barr and Isabella Barr. Amazingly, she found another revealing document that had also identified William Barr Jr. as the last slave-owner. In her fourth letter to Florence on April 9, 1977, Hazel wrote, "I hope what I am sending to you today is good news as far as tracing your ancestors. Just as I suspected, Edmond Beckley's owner was William Barr. If you will read closely the Pension Application papers that Edmond Beckley submitted . . . "[3] There was a Civil War pension application!

On July 11, 1904, Edmond applied for a pension for his service in the Confederate Army during the Civil War. On the application, the following significant questions were asked and answered:

**What is your age?** Edmond Beckley answered, "Sixty-six."

**How long have you been a bona fide resident of Mississippi?** Edmond answered, "Forty-six years." His answer confirmed that they had arrived in Mississippi by the spring of 1859. Since Edmond answered that he was sixty-six years old, and that he had been in Mississippi for forty-six of those sixty-six years, he had estimated that he was around twenty years old when he was brought to Mississippi. The 1900 census-taker recorded July 1838 as his birth month and year; therefore, he was twenty years old from July 1858 to July 1859.

**In what state did you reside when you served as a servant of a soldier or sailor in the services of the Confederate States?** Edmond answered, "Mississippi."

**When did you serve in that capacity?** Edmond answered, "1861 to 1864."

**How long did you serve?** Edmond answered, "About 3 years."

**What was the name of the party whom you served?** Edmond answered, "William Barr."

**What was the name or designation of the company and regiment or vessel in which your <u>owner</u> served?** Edmond answered, "Pontotoc Minute Men 2nd Mississippi Regiment."

**Where were you at the close of the war?** Edmond answered, "Pontotoc County."

Many of the Confederate States of America (CSA) passed laws granting pensions to indigent Confederate veterans. African-American veterans were not eligible to apply for the pensions until much later than white veterans. They had performed a multitude of war duties for the Confederacy that included serving as teamsters, shoemakers, breastworks builders, drummers, nurses, laborers, servants, cooks, and musicians.[4] In many cases, some former slaves had even served as body servants. Edmond Beckley was a body servant of William Barr Jr., who had served with the Pontotoc Minute Men, Company G, of the Second Regiment of the Mississippi Volunteers. Barr participated in the Battle of Manassas, but he was forced to retire from battle after contracting typhoid fever. He was granted a discharge for disability on November 6, 1861. However, Edmond continued his war labor duties in the Confederacy until 1864.

The 2004 Beckley Family Reunion was planned to be held in Tupelo, Mississippi the weekend of July 3rd, a week before the 2004 Reed & Puryear Family Reunion in Atlanta. Months prior, I had received a reunion letter, as well as a vocal invitation, to attend from

Ruby Beckley, the president of the Mississippi Beckley Club. Her cheerful personality was very comforting and welcoming. I was also invited to share some of my research findings with the family. I was thrilled by the invitation.

In the midst of finalizing the details for our Atlanta reunion, Cousin Leroy and I prepared to attend the Beckley reunion with much anticipation. For us, attending this reunion would be rejoicing the heart and soul of Grandpa Bill Reed, who kept Cannon Beckley close to his heart and who had shared details with Cousin Ike about their childhood relationship on the Barr farm. We would finally embrace Cannon's descendants in person. We would also be rejoicing the heart of Pleasant Barr, as the Beckleys were the descendants of his sister, Sue, who he had also been separated from. Rather he had learned of their whereabouts after 1859 – just a mere forty miles from him in Ripley – is conjecture. If they had not seen each other anymore after 1859, our attendance would, in essence, be a spiritual unification of a brother and sister.

The reunion agenda entailed a Saturday morning history reenactment of the Beckley Five to be held in Pontotoc County on the grounds of the College Hill Christian Methodist Episcopal Church, the family church that was organized in 1872. Their first pastor was Rev. Jacob C. Beckley.[5] This unique program gave family members from far and near a general history lesson about the lives of the Beckleys in rural Mississippi during the early 1900s. It also allowed family members to see the area of Pontotoc County, Mississippi where the Beckleys had settled. On the church grounds, Cousin Leroy and I lovingly embraced our Beckley cousins, including Susie, Ouida, and Vikki, who were colorfully dressed in lime green t-shirts and who had heard about our expected attendance. Several family members, Maurice Beckley especially, had a lot of questions to ask concerning my research findings in comparison with the oral history he had been told for years. Prior to the reunion, I decided that I would expound on my genealogical findings only if I was asked.

*I was delivering an impromptu history speech at the 2004 Beckley Family Reunion, Tupelo, Mississippi. Courtesy of the late Maurice Beckley*

After the history reenactment, I was invited to come up and speak to the family. I was not prepared. However, I felt the ancestors' guidance as I told the story of our family's forced separation that occurred in Abbeville, South Carolina. Tears flowed from faces, including Cousin Leroy's, while others possessed a look of wonderment, as if they were imagining the struggles that our ancestors had resiliently endured. Somehow, I managed to keep my composure.

At the banquet later that evening in Tupelo, I nervously delivered a more-prepared, brief history speech. I also provided a five-page handout that included my written version of our early history, a copy of Rev. Jacob Beckley's death certificate, the 1880 census report, the 1843 Barr inventory, and a copy of the church minutes about Jacob and Sue's dismissal from Upper Long Cane Church. I took 150 copies of the handout with me to distribute among the nearly two hundred people in attendance. I wanted to show documentation that indicated the parentage of the Beckley Five and their siblings. It was well-received by many but not by some who charged me with an impossible infraction of altering the family's history. Acceptance was going to take time; an eventual, total acceptance by everyone was probably too much to hope for.

The banquet speaker was Rust College president, Dr. David Beckley. He and Cousin Leroy had known each other as long-time colleagues who had served on various Rust College committees. In the past, they had not seen eye-to-eye on a number of issues related to the historically Black college. However, that night, despite their past disagreements, they knew each other as blood cousins, the descendants of Lewis and Fanny Barr. They knew why they had been told in college that they resemble each other. Our attendance at the 2004 reunion planted a seed of togetherness. I wondered if it would take root and grow.

An artistic sketch of "The Beckley Five" brothers, the sons of Sue. Counterclockwise from top: Edmond Beckley (1838-1906), Cannon Beckley (1840-1903), Rev. Jacob Beckley (1847-1917), Lewis Beckley (1849-1942), Henry Clay Beckley (1846-1901). Source: Beckley Family Reunion book, courtesy of Ira Blount

The gravestone of Cannon Beckley, son of Sue, who was buried at College Hill Cemetery, Pontotoc County, Mississippi. The following was inscribed, "C.C. Beckley, Died July 7, 1903, aged 63 years and 6 months."

Dr. Leroy Frazier and Dr. David Beckley, the President of Rust College, were college mates at Rust during the early 1970s, unaware that they descend from two siblings, Pleasant & Sue, who were separated during slavery in 1859.

# Chapter 11

## "Back to Caroliny"

*D*r. Martin Luther King stated, ". . . I have a dream that one day on the red hills of Georgia the sons of former slaves and the sons of former slave owners will be able to sit down together at a table of brotherhood." This happened in Abbeville, South Carolina.

*"Removed to Mississippi January 1866"* – This notation was written in the Upper Long Cane Church Session book for Alfred, a former slave of Lemuel Reid's father, Samuel. Although it pertains to another slave, it was good evidence that indicated the time of Grandpa Bill Reed's exodus from Abbeville, South Carolina, coupled with Cousin Ike Deberry's memories. He had relayed, "When Lem Reid told them that they was as free as he was, Grandpa said that they stayed on the place a little while longer to help him bring in the crops."

Samuel Reid died in 1857, and his estate record shows that Alfred was sold to his son-in-law, John R. Wilson, who lived adjacent to Lemuel. Additionally, the church records indicate that Glasgow Barr's wife and children were enslaved by the Lesleys, the same family who previously owned Jacob Beckley Sr. Robert Hall Lesley's estate record shows that a slave named Glasgow had been sold from the estate to the same John R. Wilson on December 22, 1847. Therefore, both Glasgow and Alfred were last enslaved by Wilson. This was, without a doubt, Rev. Glasgow Wilson, the son of Glasgow Barr and Grandpa Bill's first cousin, who had migrated with him and others to Mississippi shortly after slavery. Thus, January 1866 was likely when some of the recently emancipated slaves from the adjoining Wilson and Reid farms were enticed to migrate to Mississippi. Grandpa Bill left Abbeville County, never to see his birthplace again.

However, he looked back. According to Cousin Ike, Grandpa Bill always wanted to travel back to South Carolina to visit, but traveling six hundred miles to South Carolina during his elderly years would have been difficult. He stated, "He often talked about going back to Caroliny, but we didn't know where to take him. He had been gone for so long that we didn't think that he would have known anyone still back there."

Who would have been there if Grandpa Bill had actually visited during the 1920s? The Abbeville County census records gleaned some insight. He would have found Pleasant Reid, who was likely the same Pleasant also enslaved on Lemuel Reid's farm. I had not been able to determine if or how this Pleasant was a relative, but the evidence supporting a familial relationship was powerful – he carried the odd name of Grandpa Bill's father, and he and Grandpa Bill were both last owned by Lemuel. This was definitely more than just coincidental. Sorry to say, had Grandpa Bill visited Abbeville, he would have found the elderly and widowed Pleasant Reid as an inmate at the Abbeville County Penal Farm. He died there in 1924, according to his death certificate which, unfortunately, did not provide the names of his parents. That was a big disappointment.

By 1880, Pleasant Reid had married and had at least four children, Anderson, Abraham, George, and Liza. By 1910, he was a shoemaker who had his own shop in the town of Lowndnesville, located twelve miles west of Abbeville. However, by 1920, he was an inmate. What happened? I wondered. Perhaps, there were other family members and former slaves of Lemuel Reid that Grandpa Bill wanted to see if they were still alive. Cousin Ike confirmed, "I always got the impression that we may still have family back there where he came from. There were people that Grandpa wanted to see again."

On a sunny Thursday, July 8, 2004, family members who carried Grandpa Bill's blood filled a chartered bus, one van, and three vehicles and headed to Abbeville, a small town that possessed a population of just under 6,000 people, according to the 2000 census. He was finally going back home, in a manner of speaking. The trip was the grand precursor to our 2004 Reed & Puryear Family Reunion in Atlanta, Georgia. Having just attended the 2004 Beckley Family Reunion in Tupelo, Mississippi, Cousin Leroy and I, who were the organizers of the reunion, anticipated the nearly two hundred family members descending on the city for the weekend. This was the first time the reunion was held in Atlanta; therefore, we thought it to be a great opportunity to visit Abbeville as a family, to take Grandpa Bill back home. Fifty-three family members from Mississippi, Tennessee, Indiana, Illinois, Missouri, Maryland, and Arkansas arrived in Atlanta early to participate in the one-day "family roots" trip, which was only two hours and fifteen minutes away by vehicle.

If someone had expressed to me more than eight years prior that I, along with a busload of family members, would be visiting the actual place where Grandpa Bill had come from, I would have not believed it in a million years. I had never imagined it. From 1987, the year I first asked Mom about her grandfather, up until 1998, I had longed to positively nail down Grandpa Bill's origins but to no avail. In 1987, visiting that then-unknown place did not even seem remotely possible. At that time, I did not know that it was even possible to trace his history back into slavery. Now, in 2004, we were going there as a family. The trip seemed surreal to me.

As we journeyed to Abbeville, many thoughts were expressed on the bus as family members prepared for the significant visit. However, my mouth dropped when, out of the blue, Cousin Ike loudly relayed the following to me and others who sat near him, "You know, Grandpa Bill never could say 'Abbeville.' He would always say Ibbieville." This was the first time he had ever mentioned this to anyone! The trip jarred his memory. During prior conversations with Cousin Ike, Grandpa Bill's birthplace was never recalled. That day, it was. He suddenly heard Grandpa Bill's voice saying "Ibbieville." I took his startling recollection as a sign. Unquestionably, Grandpa Bill's spirit was surrounding us as the caravan of his descendants traveled up Interstate 85 towards South Carolina.

Prior to our trip, John Blythe, Rose-Marie Williams, Robert Speer, who was the President of the Abbeville Historical Society, and Jane Jefferson expressed via e-mail a great interest in making this an unforgettable homecoming event, not only for our family but for the town of Abbeville and the state of South Carolina. We had no idea that they would literally roll out the red carpet with a few surprises.

Unfortunately, Abbeville had been receiving some bad press for several months. On December 8, 2003, in a ten-hour standoff that included hundreds of officers, two officers – Abbeville County Sheriff Sergeant Danny Wilson, who is African-American, and State Constable Donnie Ouzts – were gunned down by Abbeville resident and troublemaker Steven Bixby. The standoff, which rocked the town like a major earthquake, stemmed from a land-survey dispute between the Bixbys and the South Carolina Department of Transportation (SCDOT) over property rights and rights-of-way. Ultimately, Bixby was convicted on seventeen counts including the two murders. He was also charged with kidnapping and conspiracy. He was given two death sentences for the murders and 125 years in prison on the other charges. Deemed as the Abbeville Horror, the deadly siege made national news.

But the Abbeville Horror was the more recent cloud of darkness that loomed over the quaint, historic-looking town. For almost nine decades, Abbeville had also been stained by its portrayal as a hotbed of racism as a result of the notorious 1916 lynching of Anthony Crawford. This horrific crime led to a sudden mass exodus of many of its African-American population to Evanston, Illinois, a northern suburb of Chicago. Crawford's great-great-granddaughter and Evanston resident, Doria Dee Johnson, wrote the following accounts of the day when her predecessor was unjustly and brutally murdered by a jealous white mob of Abbevillans, estimated to be between 200 and 400:

His ordeal lasted all day. His body was beaten and dragged through town to show other Negroes what would happen to them if they got "insolent." Finally, he was taken to the county fair grounds and strung up to a tree and riddled with bullets. Although we have heard his body was thrown on someone's lawn, we have yet to locate his grave. The family was ordered to vacate their land, wind up business and get out of town. They did just that. His crime you might ask: cursing a white man for offering him a low price for the cotton seed he was trying to sell and being too rich for a Negro.[1]

Born in January 1865, shortly before slavery's end, on Ben Crawford's farm just north of Abbeville, Anthony Crawford became the wealthiest African-American land-owner in Abbeville County and the surrounding areas. He had amassed 427 acres of land where he prosperously farmed cotton. According to Doria, "His holdings were at least ten percent of all land owned by Negroes in the county. He would loan whites money between harvests and had changed his crop from cotton to corn before the white farmers did because of the boll weevil."[2] Just like the Tulsa Race Riot of 1921, when over 300 African Americans were massacred and thirty-five city blocks, including a popularly known section called Black Wall Street, were burned by an angry white militia, the prominence of an African-American had become too much for many whites to handle, even the ones who had borrowed money from him.

On the morning of October 21, 1916, Crawford rode into town on his horse to W. D. Barksdale's store to sell his cottonseed. Barksdale lowballed him, offering him eight-five cents during a time when cottonseed was selling for ninety cents a bushel. During their argument, Crawford was called an "uppity nigger," and subsequently, a mob gathered, swarmed him, and lynched him. Years prior to the lynching, he had expressed to his family, "The day a white man hits me is the day I die."[3]

Abbeville had had enough of the negative images the nation was reading in articles and viewing on television. Our timely visit was considered an uplifting story with a positive message. As the bus entered Abbeville's court square around eleven that morning, we were awestruck to see white waving hands underneath a big yellow sign at one of the downtown establishments. The sign read: "Welcome to Abbeville, Reeds!" That establishment was the Rough House, a downtown store and restaurant owned and operated by Shelley Reid. Lemuel Reid was his great-great-great-grandfather. To add to our astonishment, as family members exited the bus in downtown Abbeville, we were greeted by a group of five smiling African-American women – the late Thomasina Wright, Catherine Willis, LaCorsha Turner, Ruth Howland, and Lilly Ray. They excitedly expressed, "We are Reids, too. We are your family! Welcome home!" Many eyes began to fill with tears. This prelude to an amazing homecoming was beyond my wildest imagination.

After we gathered downtown, members of the Abbeville Historical Society led the family to the Abbeville County Courthouse, where in the courtroom the family was surprisingly given a homecoming program. We were honored by the presence of several local and state dignitaries – the Abbeville County Council chairman Claude Thomas, an African-American, Abbeville Mayor Harold

*A welcome sign at "The Rough House" in downtown Abbeville, South Carolina, which is owned and operated by Shelley Reid, a descendant of Lemuel Reid.*

McNeill, noted Abbeville historian Dr. Lowry Ware, Jannie Harriot and Bernie Wright of the South Carolina African American Heritage Commission. Wright is also the executive director of the Penn Center on St. Helena Island, South Carolina, where the first school for newly freed African Americans in South Carolina was established in 1862. The program was also sponsored by the Greater Abbeville Chamber of Commerce and Operation Impact. Their involvement displayed the significance of this visit to Abbeville for the town and the state; its magnitude I was still trying to comprehend, not expecting the day to begin like it had.

The opening of the program was a recital of the Pledge of Allegiance that was led by Lemuel Reid IV, who was dressed in his Boy Scout uniform. Lemuel Reid was his great-great-great-great-grandfather. I find it amazing how life can make such ironic twists and turns – to have a young descendant of an ancestor's slave-owner, who happened to carry his name, to welcome the descendants of his ancestor's slave. At the age of ten, little Lemuel IV likely did not understand the significance of his participation at the time. Perhaps, in a few years he will. Following the pledge, a history synopsis was given by Dr. William Reid Jr., Lemuel's great-great-grandson who, ironically, was known to his family and constituents as "Bill Reid."

At the microphone, Claude Thomas marveled at the audience in the courtroom that consisted of African Americans and whites, the descendants of folk who came to America in starkly different circumstances, who were uniting in this homecoming celebration. As he welcomed the family back to Abbeville, he shared, "Despite our travel arrangements we are all in the same boat now."

To add to the excitement of the program, Mayor Harold McNeill presented Cousin Ike, Cousin Armentha, Cousin Leroy, and me, on behalf of the entire family, with the key to the city of Abbeville. Attempting to loosen up a family who was still in a state of shock from all that had transpired thus far, he facetiously expressed, "It'll open up everything but the bank." His banter worked; laughter from the audience erupted, putting the audience more at ease. He also read aloud a proclamation honoring our journey back to Abbeville. John Blythe later revealed, "The idea about the key to the city came from the Mayor himself. We asked for the proclamation, but he took it a step further. And you should know that's not a common practice."

Cousin Leroy brought two white roses that we saw befitting to present to Lemuel Reid's descendants. Although white roses symbolize purity and innocence, the roses that were presented to the Reid Family represented a necessary healing for our families. We could not deny what happened during slavery in Abbeville County. More importantly, we shall never forget. American slavery was inhumane and had been, unfortunately, the integral part of the nation's economy for over two centuries. However, we can live with the past without being lugged down by it. The roses symbolized that we have moved on in harmony, allowing the past to pave a highway towards a brighter future. The roses also meant that we came to Abbeville with peace and with love, possessing no feelings of ill will in our hearts against the descendants of those that had oppressed our ancestors.

Shelley Reid approached the microphone and accepted the roses from Cousin Leroy, a great-great-grandson of Grandpa Bill Reed, who was a former slave his great-great-great-grandfather had purchased from his Barr relatives. Carbon-copying his mother, wife, and uncles to an e-mail he sent to us several days later, he shared the following, "I was personally very touched by y'all's very kind gesture of presenting flowers to Lemuel and Sophia Weston Reid. We thought it important to place them at their graves in Upper Long Cane cemetery."[4] A picture of the roses on their graves was attached to the e-mail. Some people could not comprehend what the roses had signified.

As a great finale to a phenomenal program, Cousin Ike, who was just three months away from his 90th birthday, approached the microphone with a happy spirit that radiated across the courtroom. The trip to Abbeville meant more to him than any other trips that he had taken in his eighty-nine years. As the oldest-living grandchild of Grandpa Bill Reed, he was visiting the source of his grandfather's stories that were shared underneath his sycamore tree, something that he had never fathomed. With pride and joy, he delivered the following impromptu speech:

> "Well, first thing I want to say is good evening to everybody. You know it's good just to come back where Grandpa started from. I used to sit and listen to him talk. He couldn't say Abbeville, he'll say Ibbieville is where he come from. He talked a whole lot about him plowing and riding with the boss man over the pasture. He said the boss man had a saddling horse, and he'll put him up behind 'em to open the gates for 'em. He said he'll get down and open the gate and they'll get back up behind the man. The man's name was Reed. I'm glad that I was able to come to see where Grandpa Bill started at. It's just a mystery to me that he came to

Senatoby, and did so well, and he couldn't read nor write. That's the reason why I like the song, somebody may remember Gladys Knight singing a song about Daddy couldn't read and Daddy couldn't write but one thing about Daddy, he sho would do right."

Laughter and applause erupted from the audience. Cousin Ike continued confidently:

"I think about that a whole lot. Grandpa lived a Christian life. My father died when I was 12 years old. My mother had 11 chil'ren, and we moved back to Grandpa's, and we stayed with Grandpa until I married. I married when I was 22 years old, so all that time from 12 until to 22, I spent it there on Grandpa's place. He learnt me a whole lot. And I tell ya another thing he learnt me, he learnt me how to behave myself."

The audience erupted in laughter again. Public-speaking was indeed his forte, and the audience was enjoying him tremendously. He continued:

"Anytime he spanked you, you can bet one thing, you had been spanked! But now, he was a Christian man. At Bulow (Beulah) Church, he'll sit and talk about how they cut logs and built that log church there. He was just, I'm going to just tell you the truth, you ought to look at his offsprings and everything; how many preachers and different things that done come out of that family. Grandpa was a man. He wasn't no put-on. Bill Reed, he was just Bill Reed. I was just thinking about Grandpa, he had a sorghum mill. You know a sorghum mill where you cook molasses. And he had a fella cooking the molasses, and they would give the person three gallons, call it Tobe, and give the Miller the fourth gallon. So when they wind up and got all the molasses out, on that third gallon, they'll give the man, I forgot his name, Wilson or something, they'll give him his two quarts and that left one quart. They'll say, 'What we gone do with this other quart? Brother Bill, what we gone do with this other quart?' Grandpa was sitting there in a chair, I never will forget that. He got up and said, 'Ain't it mine! Well dag gonnit, put that in my barrel if it's mine! I won't nothing of nobody's else but mines!'"

The audience laughed as he mocked his grandfather. Cousin Ike continued, fascinating the audience with his memory:

"He was an honest man. After all, that was his quart. Wasn't but a quart but it was his'em. I look out over this thing and I see so many faces and think about so much family. One night, I was sitting up, trying my best to count the preachers that done come out that Reed Family. I got lost cause some of them I missed, cause I got two and I missed them two!"

Laughter followed again. Cousin Ike continued:

"I ain't gone kill too much time. I'm gone sang just a lil verse of a song for Grandpa. The work I done speak for me. So I'm just gone sing a verse or two of it."

Cousin Ike commenced to singing a verse of the same old Negro spiritual he had sung when he spotted the sycamore tree during our visit out to the Old Home Place.

To add to the overflow of ironies that had been unfolding, Rev. Jeffrey Lang of the Upper Long Cane Presbyterian Church, the same church where Rev. William Barr had ministered and the same church where our enslaved ancestors attended, gave the benediction and the blessing to conclude the program. The next stop was the Reid Place.

Mayor Harold McNeill presented the Reed Family with a Key to the City of Abbeville, South Carolina, July 8, 2004.

Cousin Isaac (Ike) Deberry and Cousin Armentha Reed Puryear standing on the porch where Lemuel Reid announced to their grandfather and the other slaves in 1865 that they were free.

In anticipation of our visit, John Blythe had diligently identified the location of Rev. Barr's farm. His efforts were tireless; the entire visit would not have happened in the colossal manner in which it had if it had not been for his willingness and enthusiasm. The Barr farm home had long since been demolished. The property, which had vastly become wooded land, had gone through several owners since 1866, when William Barr Jr. sold the last tract of land to William Tully Branch. Nevertheless, Pecan Road, located just two miles north of the Abbeville city limits, meandered through the property. It was our out-of-the-way detour on the way to the Reid Place.

The Reid Place was less than two miles away from the Barr farm, so we arrived there within minutes. Full of excitement, we exited the bus. We had come back – one hundred and thirty-eight years later. Accompanying us were Lemuel Reid's descendants, some of whom had never stepped foot inside the Reid Place. It was not the kind of mansion I had seen on *Gone with the Wind* or other southern plantation houses. It was plainer and skinnier. The pale, empty two-story house was coolly shaded by several large, very old oak trees – trees that Grandpa Bill probably planted. Two chimneys, one on each side, stood tall, with one bearing a large crack that was caused by the Charleston earthquake of 1886. Thankfully, the current owner, Bobby Bowen, allowed us to walk the grounds to explore some of the remnants of our family history and to walk over the very same land that Grandpa Bill had plowed as a slave. The blood, sweat, and tears of our ancestor were in that soil.

Built in 1861, the house had reached a dilapidated state because it had been unoccupied since 1995. I was disappointed at its condition but very grateful that it was still there. It was an echoing shell; its vibrancy had long vanished. According to Wayne Reid, previous residents had died from cancer, and the Bowens had been concerned about the possibility of some type of cancer-causing material in the home; they refrained from moving in it themselves after they acquired the property. I couldn't help but wonder if Grandpa Bill's spirit had somehow miraculously interrupted a decision to demolish it, knowing that one day his descendants would be walking the grounds, understanding their history, and strengthening family ties. As we walked through the home, we marveled at how long and well it held up, although in its deteriorating condition. Cousin Bill Reed, who is Grandpa Bill's namesake and great-grandson, expressed with amazement, "Look at what my ancestors built!"

As I stood on the grounds of the Reid Place, I envisioned that gloomy day that Lemuel brought him and possibly others there from the Barr farm. I envisioned Grandpa Bill working hard in the fields, plowing the bottom land with the other slaves. I envisioned him opening the gates for Lemuel for him to ride over the pasture. I envisioned him with a shovel walking towards a hill near the place with Lemuel to bury his gold during the Civil War. I envisioned him helping the other slaves construct the house, working from "can't to can't." Although the slave cabins had been demolished many years ago, I envisioned him in one of the cabins with Mariah, the older sister he had told Cousin Ike about, probably the one who took care of him after he was forever separated from his parents. I envisioned the day a man from Mississippi came on the place and clandestinely told him and others about having a better life back in Panola County, Mississippi, where there were "fat pigs running around with apples in their mouths." I envisioned him and the others walking away, never to return to the Reid Place physically but spiritually through us – his descendants.

Walking up the crumbling steps to the porch, Cousin Ike stated, "I never thought in a million years that I would get to stand on these steps." His grandfather had told him about those steps. On those steps of that porch in 1865, Lemuel announced to the twenty-plus slaves, "Y'all are as free as I am." A century and three scores later, the grandchildren of one of those slaves had returned. Led by the spirit of the ancestors, the family sang in unison a few verses of *We Have Come This Far By Faith* – an appropriate song for the historical occasion. As we sung, we knew that Grandpa Bill had remained with us since we had left Atlanta earlier that morning.

Before departing Abbeville, we were informed that a big, scrumptious meal was waiting on us at the Abbeville Civic Center. This was a big surprise. This was not part of our itinerary, but we would have been very inhospitable, according to Southern customs, to not partake in a down-home, Southern meal that had been prepared especially for us. To our sheer delight, Catherine Willis, her daughter Thomasina, Thomasina's daughter, LaCorsha, and Catherine's first cousin, Ruth Howland, had prepared turnip greens, macaroni and cheese, green beans, baked chicken, ham, cake, peach cobbler, and sweet tea. Our visit to Abbeville was not only momentous for us, but it meant a lot to them. Only having a few relatives there Abbeville from her father's family, Catherine had often wondered if she had more relatives somewhere. She had always wanted to be part of a big family. Days before our arrival, they had read in the *Press and Banner*, the local Abbeville newspaper, about our visit and were very excited to welcome us as their cousins. We felt their love. Ruth expressed to us, "Y'all are family that we never knew we had. Our grandmother would never forgive us if we had let y'all come to town and didn't see that y'all got a good meal."

Catherine and Ruth are the granddaughters of Cunningham and Susie Reid Lee. On September 7, 1897, Susie was born just a stone's throw away from the Reid Place just north of Abbeville; therefore, chances are great that she was the daughter or the granddaughter of a slave once owned by Lemuel Reid or his father and Rebecca Barr's brother, Samuel Reid. When they told me the name of their grandmother, and hearing them say "Susie," chills went through me like flowing water. The ancestors were speaking to us, again. Sue and Susie were family names. In my mind, I was saying, "They have to be our blood kin some kind of way!" Although a consanguineous connection had not been positively determined, we felt in our hearts that one existed. Shortly after our visit, Catherine expressed the following via e-mail:

Dear Family,

I was very happy to see you all. That made my day to see all my cousins. I want to get to know every one of my cousins. That was a dream come true for us to meet. I'd wondered where all my father's people were because no one but Ruth and her brother and myself were left here. Ruth is the only one who could tell us something about the family. All of the old people died before I got to know any of them. My father Edward Lee left Abbeville when I was a baby but he kept in touch with my mother so he would always know where I was. Daddy told me he left here one night walking. All he had was what he had on his back and he never came back until grandmother Susie died. I am happy God brought us together. That was nothing but the hands of God working in this family. All I can say is Thank You Jesus and I pray that God will keep us in His hands.[5]

Susie's descendants had also extended an invitation to Lemuel Reid's descendants. While we all – black Reeds and white Reids – sat there in the civic center, enjoying one of the tastiest meals I had eaten in a long time and chatting about the great day we all just experienced, I was reminded of a line from Dr. Martin Luther King's *I Have A Dream* speech that he delivered on August 28, 1963 at the Lincoln Memorial in Washington, D.C. He stated, "I have a dream that one day on the red hills of Georgia the sons of former slaves and the sons of former slave owners will be able to sit down together at a table of brotherhood." Sixteen miles east of the Georgia-South Carolina state line, this happened in Abbeville, South Carolina on July 8, 2004.

As the caravan headed out of Abbeville on its way back to Atlanta, a feeling of incompletion came over me. I felt that this would not and should not be our only visit. I didn't know when, and I didn't know why, but I knew that we and many others would return. There was more that needed to happen. The ancestors were trying to tell me something. Things had not come full circle. That feeling was just there, and it wouldn't go away.

*White roses were placed on the graves of Lemuel & Sophia Reid, Upper Long Cane Cemetery, Abbeville, South Carolina. Courtesy of Shelley Reid*

*The Reid Family – the descendants of Lemuel Reid. Left to right: Melanie Reid (wife of Oscar), Joel Reid (son of Oscar), Marilyn Reid (mother of Oscar and Shelley), Oscar Reid, Hannah Reid (daughter of Oscar), Lemuel Reid (son of Oscar), and Shelley Reid.*

Group picture taken at the Abbeville Civic Center, July 8, 2004

*Amused by Cousin Ike Deberry's humor in his presentation, I am seated next to Angela Walton-Raji, whose great-great-grandmother, Amanda Young, married Pleasant Barr in Ripley, Mississippi shortly after the Civil War.*

# *Chapter 12*

## "Let No Man Put Asunder."

*I*n 2004, for the first time in my life, I felt myself spiraling down a path towards depression. For eleven years, genealogy had been my emotional and psychological refuge, but it was not enough to combat the unhappiness of rising every morning and going to work in a career that was no longer self-fulfilling. The mistake of choosing a career for financial reasons rather than pursuing my true passions had finally caught up with me. I no longer wanted to be a civil engineer, and I knew that my passion for history would feed a history-related career. But I did not know what to do. I began to have thoughts of just walking away from my career, but having a mortgage, a car note, and other bills dictated that I continued to wake up every morning and head to work at a private engineering firm in Memphis, Tennessee until I executed another plan. But what was the plan? I was clueless, and that uncertainty was causing days of sadness in the midst of a busy year.

For the 2004 Reed & Puryear Family Reunion, Cousin Leroy and I decided to add a tour of Atlanta to the reunion itinerary. Having picnics in the park in the Southern heat and humidity was becoming more undesirable for many family members; therefore, we felt that a bus tour to various city attractions would be a great alternative. The family had enjoyed a bus tour of Chicago for our 2002 reunion. In retrospect, planning a one-day "family roots" trip to Abbeville, South Carolina and also including a tour of the city on the reunion itinerary will be something I will not ever do again. This worked us to death, in a manner of speaking. The reunion itinerary also included a "Get-Acquainted" Reception on Friday evening, an evening banquet after the city tour on Saturday, and a worship service at the hotel on Sunday morning.

During that tour of Atlanta, a light bulb went off inside my head. As our three-bus caravan passed the Auburn Avenue Research Library on African-American Culture and History near downtown, with me marveling at the "on African-American Culture and History" part of its name, I got an overwhelming feeling that I needed to be in Atlanta. The city was known for its vibrancy in African-American life and culture, as well as other cultures, and its frequent hosting of culture-related events – much more than Memphis. I wanted to make Atlanta my new home.

Three months later, I courageously placed my two-year-old Southaven, Mississippi brick home on the market, happily ended my eight-year career as an engineer, eagerly packed up all of my belongings, and expeditiously moved to Atlanta – in that order. Classes were scheduled to begin on Wednesday, January 12, 2005, and my God-sent cousin, Bettina Reed, rented me a room in her two-story home in suburban Austell that she shared with her brother, Kelvin. I had enrolled into the African-American Studies graduate program at Clark Atlanta University to begin my transition into a new and fulfilling career. I took a leap of Faith, giving up the comforts of a new, three-bedroom house in suburbia, a decent salary, and other luxuries. But those things had become insignificant. My happiness was much more important. That bold move turned out to be one of the best decisions I had ever made. It prevented me from falling deeply into a state of depression. I later realized that this move was part of my ancestors' plan.

A year and a half later, the other reason why I needed to be in Atlanta was revealed to me. There was something that my ancestors wanted – a "coming together" reunion. God was their overseer to make sure that it happened. This became evident to me on Sunday evening, July 23, 2006, a week after the 2006 Reed & Puryear Family Reunion in Pensacola, Florida. That day, I found myself in deep reflection about the reunion-packed summer I had just experienced. Shortly after moving to Atlanta, Amelia Jefferson, the president of the newly-formed Atlanta Beckley Club, and Ouida Howard invited me to join the family club. I was honored by their invitation, and I immediately accepted it. The club diligently planned the 49th Annual Beckley Family Reunion that was held in Atlanta, Georgia the weekend of June 30th. Approximately 200 family members attended. At the same time, several cousins and I were assisting our cousin, Machelle Reed Easley, a great-great-granddaughter of Grandpa Bill, with the plans for our 2006 reunion. Like the 2006 Beckley Family Reunion, the 2006 Reed & Puryear Family Reunion was held in a city it had never been held before. Nearly 180 family members made the sojourn to the panhandle of Florida to attend that reunion.

Over a course of three weeks, I had been in the presence of nearly four hundred family members who all shared a profound and historical commonality. Flowing through our veins was the blood of Lewis and Fanny Barr. That Sunday, the reality of this bond was so overwhelming that I could not think about anything else. The ancestors were speaking; they wanted their descendants to unite. Slavery had torn us apart, and the time was approaching to mend the broken ties in a grand fashion.

How would I pull this off? Would the families even go for the idea? I also wondered if I had the energy to do it. After spending a summer working diligently with two reunion committees, I was tired.

I was ready to pass the reunion planning torch on to other family members. Planning a family reunion is a very laborious task, undeniably a labor of love. For future reunions, I only desired to attend rather than being heavily involved with the logistics of the reunion itinerary. But, that Sunday, I felt that my work was not over. So I sat at my laptop and allowed my ancestors to guide my fingers across the keyboard. To put the idea in family members' minds, I wrote the following and e-mailed it to the Beckley Family e-mail list with the subject heading entitled "Moment of Reflection:"

Hello Family,

I just had to take this moment of time to reflect. As a lover of African-American history, I often sit back and wonder what our ancestors were like, what they looked like, what they had to endure during American slavery, which was one of the cruelest forms of slavery this world has ever seen. Through the 300+ years of remarkable resilience and profound endurance, they emerged out of that "dark cloud" as strong as ever, and we must continue to pass on their mental and physical strength. As far back as we can go, all of our ancestors of African/African-American descent deserve recognition, and the generations now and tomorrow should know about them. Would you not want your great-great-great-great-granddaughter/niece/nephew to know about your existence?

I enjoyed the 2006 Beckley Family Reunion, and I am thrilled beyond measure of the Atlanta Beckley Club for accepting and welcoming me unconditionally. With the spirit of our ancestors in mind, it was a pleasure being a part of you guys! Thanks again for executing that unity that our ancestors wanted us to have. Slavery tried to divide us physically and mentally, but you guys broke down that barrier of mental slavery that sometimes continues to be a dividing mechanism among our people today, and for that, I am proud to be a part of you guys!

Like I said earlier, I often wonder about the ancestors. During their time on Rev. William H. Barr's farm in Abbeville, South Carolina during the early 1800s, Lewis & Fanny Barr were able to unite and start a family in the midst of the great challenges and unspeakable injustices of chattel slavery they faced. Through the love they found in each other, they produced your ancestor, Sue, my ancestor, Pleasant, and several other children. And as I experienced the wonderful Beckley Family Reunion on the 30th of June in Georgia and the exciting Reed Family Reunion on July 14th in Florida, it became quite apparent to me that the importance of family and unity is very prominent among Lewis & Fanny Barr's direct descendants. During those two reunion weekends, rest assured that they were smiling and saying to each other, "Honey, look at what we produced. Oh, how happy we are that y'all are calling our names!"

Maybe one day, before I become a senior citizen, we can make them even happier by coming together and combating what slavery tried to do to us. Unity is in our blood. If anyone needs to be reminded of that, just look at the Beckley Reunion Photo Gallery and the Reed Reunion Photo Gallery. The spirit of reunion is shining bright! Thanks for allowing me to share this reflection.[1]

Minutes after the e-mail was sent, the ancestors began to reveal more – 2009 should be the year it is held. Some people have asked, "How do you know when there are other forces nudging at you or speaking to you?" My explanation is simple. Voices are not actually heard. But for me, I can be thinking about something one minute, such as school, a current event, or something I had just seen on television.

Then suddenly, the next minute, a thought enters my mind that is totally unrelated to what I had just been thinking. Then, what follows is an inner feeling or gut instinct that the sudden thought should be carried out, no matter what. That's how I know.

By the spring of 1859, the children and grandchildren of Lewis and Fanny Barr had been torn apart from each other. Grandpa Bill was sold to Lemuel Reid; his father Pleasant Barr was sold and taken to Ripley, Mississippi, and Pleasant's sister, Sue Beckley, and most of her children were taken to Pontotoc County, Mississippi. Grandpa Bill laid the foundation for a special reunion when he told Cousin Ike about his close relationship with his cousin, Cannon Beckley, to whom he had waved goodbye as Cannon, his siblings, parents, and their grandmother, Fanny Barr, were being taken away. The year 2009 would be 150 years later. It made sense! That had to be the year when this "coming together" reunion should happen, and we had to go back to the place where we were last together as a cohesive family – Abbeville, South Carolina. There was now a clearer reason why I had a feeling of incompletion as we were leaving Abbeville in July 2004. This meant that I had three years to make this a reality. I wondered if I was up for the challenge.

Four hours later, Cannon Beckley's great-great-grandson, Kenneth Johnson, responded to the e-mail, "Melvin, you pose a very good question to answer. At what point are we to unite as the Reed/Beckley or Beckley/Reed or Barr family reunion? I like it! We owe it to our ancestors to answer this question. We were separated by slavery, but now we have the power to right a wrong. WILL WE DO IT?"[2] Kenneth had heard the call as well. His response gave me hope.

More e-mail responses supporting the idea followed. Some family members even offered to assist with the planning. I sent a similar e-mail to the Reed Family e-mail list, and favorable responses followed as well. However, the reluctant and unenthusiastic ones chose not to voice their concerns over e-mail. There was a reason. The year 2009 was slated to be the year that the Chicago Beckley Club would host the

52nd Annual Beckley Family Reunion. This particular reunion was one that many family members were eagerly awaiting. In their reunion history, the Chicago reunions were always some of the family's highest attended and highly anticipated reunions, and the last one was in 2002. Many Chicagoans were ready for it to come back to their city; they were ready to party on Michigan Avenue.

After consideration from the Chicago Beckley Club, who held a special meeting to discuss the proposal, they voted unanimously to not forego their 2009 reunion. I was bewildered. Did they not see the historical significance of a "coming together" reunion? Was partying on Michigan Avenue far greater than mending fractured ties 150 years after those ties were broken? Did they not read how we had the chance to repair the damage that slavery had caused? For me and for Lewis and Fanny, postponing a "coming together" reunion on the 150th year anniversary of the involuntary separation was not an option.

The Chicago club wanted to extend an invitation to the Reeds – the descendants of Pleasant Barr – to attend the 2009 Beckley Family Reunion. They encouraged us to become part of the "Beckley Experience." The gesture was nice, but frankly, I was disappointed. Other Beckleys outside of Chicago expressed disappointment as well. I decided to keep the club's unanimous decision a secret from the Reeds. I did not even tell my mother – Grandpa Bill Reed's youngest granddaughter. This was a strategic and necessary decision. I did not want Pleasant Barr's descendants to harbor ill feelings towards his sister Sue Beckley's descendants before they got a chance to reunite. That would have been detrimental to the cause. Their decision had the potential to dampen the enthusiasm and hope for a "coming together" reunion, and I could not let that happen. I responded to their decision with the following message to their e-mail list, "As a tribute to our ancestors who were torn apart from each other, we will move forward to pay homage to them for paving the way and to recognize their struggles that we can only imagine. I am sure they would want a grand, one-time reunion in 2009 to mark the 150th-year of their forced separation . . ."

My intentions of moving forward were made clear. The club's decision would not deter the efforts to rejoice the hearts of Lewis, Fanny, and the rest of our ancestors. Their decision just meant that once the "coming together" reunion was planned for 2009, the Beckleys would have to make a choice to either attend both reunions or attend only one of them. Since the summer of 2009 was three years away, perhaps there would be a change of heart. The ancestors wanted to see this reunion come to fruition; therefore, I gave the idea what it needed – time. For the next two years, I remained silent about it and concentrated on completing my thesis to obtain my Master's degree in African-American Studies. However, the ancestors did not allow time to lessen my desire to see this reunion take place. It was far too important for that to happen.

The year 2008 arrived so swiftly that I hardly remembered the year 2007. Indeed, it is funny how time flies. As I had anticipated, the thoughts of the special "coming together" reunion had not been buried after the idea was presented in 2006. In fact, the thought of it became a nuisance because I could not let it go. Now, the summer of 2008 had arrived, and it was time to put some plans in motion quickly if the reunion was going to happen in 2009. The Reeds had just enjoyed another bi-annual family reunion in July in Nashville, Tennessee, another new location. To our delight, 205 family members tackled the high gas prices and traveled to middle Tennessee. Also, the Beckleys had just enjoyed their 51st annual reunion in St. Louis, Missouri, the fourth time it had been held there since their first St. Louis reunion in 1987.

I soon contacted Amelia, who had offered in 2006 to assist with the planning. Thankfully, she was still on board, despite her busy schedule as an assistant principal and attending Clark Atlanta University part-time to obtain her Ph.D. An e-mail was soon sent to members of the Atlanta Beckley Club, and to my joy, Ouida and three other club members, Denise Harrington, Jerilyn Beckley, and Frank Turpin, excitedly volunteered to assist as well, despite their own busy schedules. From Las Vegas, Vikki Jenkins eagerly volunteered, vowing to do as much as she could from two thousand miles away. Also, Cousin Leroy and our cousin, Clara King, who also reside in Atlanta, were on board. Clara's great-grandmother was Grandpa Bill Reed's sister, Mary Pratt. Cousin Leroy, Cousin Clara, and I were the Pleasant Barr branch of the motivated, nine-people planning team whose enthusiasm inspired me even more.

On Sunday, July 27, 2008, we gathered at Cousin Leroy's house in Stone Mountain for our first official meeting. One would have thought that the nine of us had known each other all of our lives. The love and excitement were so thick that no one could have sliced it with a machete. We were there for a great purpose; one that none of us had ever heard of. Having served as the online forum board manager of AfriGeneas.com's Family Reunion Forum for over five years, I read many accounts of successful and unique family reunions that had taken place across the country among African Americans. However, I had never heard of a reunion of two families, who had been totally oblivious of each other's existence, coming together on the 150th-year anniversary of when their ancestors were separated during slavery. When I expressed to colleagues and friends about the plan and purpose of our special reunion, I typically got a one-word, initial response – "Wow!"

As we convened, we realized that we were faced with a huge challenge – the economy. This was not foreseen when I e-mailed the idea in 2006, at least not foreseen or fore-heard with my eyes and ears. However, the signs of a deteriorating economy became prevalent shortly afterwards. The home foreclosure epidemic began in late 2006, with many people losing their homes to foreclosures left and right. By 2008, the nation was seeing some of its highest home foreclosure rates ever. This was partially caused by many people losing their jobs and the bad results of subprime mortgage loaning. Many businesses were going bankrupt, and many private employers were cutting payrolls, causing nearly ten percent of America's work force to become unemployed. The nation was bracing for some of its highest unemployment rates in years. We were in a recession. All of this was occurring while Illinois senator Barack Hussein Obama II, the son of an African father from Kenya and a white mother from Kansas, was running to become the nation's first African-American president. We went into our first official meeting predicting that the nation's economic woes would negatively affect the attendance. However, we decided to press on. There would not ever be another 150th-year anniversary in our lifetime, so postponement was unspeakable.

With the ancestors' spirits surrounding us, the first meeting was phenomenal. A date was determined, the name of the "coming together" reunion was unanimously agreed upon, some duties were assigned, and a theme was decided – all within a matter of two hours. We had also decided to have monthly meetings up until the reunion to finalize the myriad of other details. Additionally, we decided, without any hesitation at all, that the start-up money to get the ball rolling would come from our own pockets. It was set. The 150th Year Commemorative Reunion of the Descendants of Lewis and Fanny Barr would monumentally take place the weekend of August 7, 8, and 9, 2009, in Atlanta, Georgia and Abbeville, South Carolina. Our theme was appropriately entitled, "Mending Family Ties, Rejoicing the Hearts of our Ancestors." The ancestors were pleased.

Friday, August 7, 2009 arrived. Despite the bad economy, 236 family members had pre-registered, and sixteen unexpected family members arrived at the Westin Hotel that day, hoping to register at the door. Although the registration deadline had long passed, we squeezed them in. Turning anyone away from a reunion of this magnitude was something that we just could not do. During the planning, we had previously targeted an attendance of around 150, despite the economy. We were feeling ambitious. However, we would have been pleased to have 100 family members in attendance, with nice representation from Reeds and Beckleys. Instead, we got 252. We were happy! Many of Sue Barr Beckley's descendants had chosen to forego their Chicago reunion and come to Atlanta to take part in this once-in-a-lifetime event. Although some absences from the Pleasant Barr branch surprised Cousin Leroy and me, we were overwhelmingly grateful for the ones that had placed this special reunion in their budgets. Equally, we were grateful for the ones who were not able to attend but were there in spirit.

Disheartened, I realized that there were family members who just did not get it. They were listening but not hearing, watching but not seeing. Although this reunion was a different one, it was just another reunion to them. The historical significance did not matter enough to attend, even though some could have afforded the trip to Atlanta.

During the eleven years I had been heavily involved in the planning of family reunions, I had also realized that for some, attending a family reunion which would be comprised of primarily new faces did not seem enticing. I could never understand that. I always felt that family reunions are about meeting lots of new kin as well as reuniting with familiar kin. Nevertheless, I realized that some people with introverted personalities are less likely to attend family reunions, despite the significance of them, unless they would be accompanied by family members that they knew. They were complacent dwelling in their "temple of familiarity," which meant that interaction with blood strangers was minimal. Sadly, there are a plethora of other reasons why some people avoided family reunions – some psychological. I became burned out from trying to convince uninterested relatives about what they were missing and the importance of family reunions.

Thankfully, the excitement of this commemorative reunion greatly overshadowed the momentary disappointment I had felt from the surprisingly-absent family members. Some later realized the importance and impact of the reunion after it happened, through the eyes of those who attended it. But when August 7th arrived, it did not matter who actually attended and which family tree branches represented more. Once all of us 252 had gathered, we were all one gigantic family, paying homage to our common ancestors and mending the family ties that were broken 150 years ago. That was the goal, and it was achieved in a grand fashion.

All of the many details that we had worried about worked themselves out perfectly. Clearly, God was in control, and our ancestors were his aides. The excitement in family members' eyes was equivalent to a child who was happy to receive a piece of his favorite candy. Within weeks leading up to the grand event, I had gotten a number of e-mails from family members who stated, "I can't wait!" The skepticism that some Beckleys had possessed several years earlier had vanished. I was informed that there were family members in attendance who initially did not accept the facts I had uncovered when I first appeared on the scene. It took time for acceptance to happen for many. For the ones that just could not accept it, they were out of sight and out of mind on that weekend – a time for togetherness.

On Friday afternoon, the planning team was busy at the registration tables, passing out name-tags, t-shirts, registration bags, and diligently registering the larger-than-expected attendance. In the midst of working, we witnessed lots of hugging, laughing, smiling, and dialoguing in lieu of the wall-size family tree that was strategically placed near the registration tables. As folk gathered in the lobby to check-in, family connections were being explained, the family history was being discussed, introductions were being made, and a beaucoup of digital pictures were being taken. The broken ties were being mended.

The first event was the "Coming Together" Commemorative Program at the hotel on Friday night. Because of the attendance, we required the usage of the hotel's grand ballroom, which was beautifully decorated with the selected colors of lavender, black, and white. The program's opening was a welcoming historical skit that was performed by Ouida and me. We played the role of Lewis and Fanny as an elderly couple who was thrilled to see the descendants of their daughter, Sue, and their son, Pleasant, together.

Jovially, as I ad-libbed my part, I looked at Aunt Eartha, turned to Ouida and said, while pointing to my beautiful aunt, "Fanny, baby, look at her! Don't she look just like our boy, Pleas!" The welcome skit generated lots of laughter, but family members were fully aware of the seriousness of it. The following lines were not scribbled on my cue card, but I was suddenly led to say to the wall-to-wall room of descendants, "It don't matter what last names we's ended up taking. Y'all have the blood of me and Fanny flowing inside of ya, and dat's what makes us a fam'lee." Our patriarch was speaking through me, and I was honored to allow him.

The program also included a PowerPoint history presentation, singing, and last but not least, eating. Good food is always essential for a great event. An inspiring message was delivered by Lucia Fernandes, a native of Angola, which was one of our confirmed African homelands. A practitioner of Capoeira Angola, an Afro-Brazilian art form that combines elements of martial arts, music, and dance, Lucia had been residing in the United States since 1999. She was the president of ASSANGA – the Association of Angolans in Georgia. Her presence at the reunion was powerful, and she was rightfully embraced as a member of the family.

In 2006, at the Reed & Puryear Family Reunion, family members had learned from DNA testing that Lewis's paternal lineage originated in Angola, in West-Central Africa. Uncle John "Sonny" Reed had submitted the DNA cheek samples because he carried the Y-chromosome of Lewis via his son, Pleasant Barr, via Pleasant's son, Grandpa Bill Reed, and via Grandpa Bill's son, his father, Granddaddy Simpson Reed. That same Y-chromosome had even been passed down unchanged from Lewis's paternal grandfather, who is believed to be the first African in his direct paternal line that touched American soil. After a long march from his Angola village, and being packed tightly with other Africans in the belly of a slave ship, he – whose name we may never uncover – endured the gruesome Middle Passage and was probably disembarked in Charleston, South Carolina sometime between 1710 and 1739. He was forced into slavery on a South Carolina plantation. Two generations later, Lewis was born into slavery sometime around 1780.

Prior to 1739, Angola-Congo Africans had comprised of nearly 70 percent of the Africans imported into South Carolina. Nearly 30,000 of the African-based population of 39,000 in South Carolina by 1739 had derived from West-Central Africa.[3] But, the Stono Rebellion had discouraged South Carolina planters from importing more Africans from that region. On September 9, 1739, twenty South Carolina Africans, most who were primarily from the Angola-Congo region, had met at the Stono River near Charleston to rebel against slavery. They burned seven plantations and killed twenty whites. They were soon captured and killed. Several of the killed Africans were decapitated; their heads were placed on mile markers along the route of the rebellion to send a threat to those who would consider planning future uprisings. Afterwards, Angola-Congo Africans were feared, and the importation of live human bodies from that region into South Carolina came to a screeching halt. They had possessed more of resilience and a determination that they were not going to be enslaved.

DNA test results had also revealed that our African ancestor was from the Mbundu people of northern Angola. The DNA results were very strong – a 100 percent match. Lucia was an Mbundu who told us about our people from whom we had descended from. This was life-changing. With family members glued to her every word, thirsty for knowledge that was coming from an actual Angolan, she shared in her speech, "You are African . . . We are one people . . . if you don't know who you are, others will define you." Heads nodded in agreement.

Adding to the thrill of the night, more African roots were revealed to the family. We did not only mend the broken ties of our family tree on this side of the Atlantic Ocean; we had also learned about our rich heritages on the other side of the Atlantic Ocean. DNA technology had been used to also uncover the maternal African roots of Fanny Barr. Luckily, the planning team was able to locate a direct descendant of Fanny who carries her mitochondrial DNA (mtDNA). This cousin was Tommy Lynn Hutchinson of Rochester, New York.

Fanny's mtDNA was passed down to all of her children, but only her daughters would pass it down, since females transfer the mtDNA in a continuous genetic chain to their children and so forth. Among her daughter Sue Beckley's descendants is where we found Tommy Lynn – the daughter of Estelle Beckley, the granddaughter of Hattie Beckley, the great-granddaughter of Louvenia Beckley, the great-great-granddaughter of Sue Beckley, and the great-great-great-granddaughter of Fanny. Like Uncle Sonny had done, she swabbed the inner cheeks of her mouth to collect DNA samples, and the samples were shipped to African Ancestry, Inc. in Silver Springs, Maryland to be analyzed. By way of video, the company's co-founder and renowned geneticist, Dr. Rick Kittles, read the following DNA results to the family, "I am happy to announce that the descendants of Fanny Barr share maternal genetic ancestry with the Fulani and Yoruba peoples of Nigeria."

A happy applause from the crowd erupted. The African roots of both Lewis and Fanny Barr had been revealed to over 200 of their descendants who amazingly had come together. This was phenomenal. We had bridged the gap between our American history and our African history. We could now claim Angola and Nigeria as our ancestral African homelands.

Immediately after Dr. Kittles' major announcement, Dallas, Texas model Ze-Enna Jenkins, a great-great-great-granddaughter of Cannon Beckley, excitedly posted the following to her Facebook profile via her cellular phone, "I'm sooo full right now! We just learned who our ancestors are! *tears* We are descendants of the Fulani and Yoruba people from Nigeria! Thank God."

To add to her joy of ancestral discovery, she immediately received the following response from one of her Facebook friends who was from

Nigeria, "Wow! That is great. What a mix! You're from the south-north. Welcome Sister! I am from Nigeria, and I love the Fulanis!"

Tears flowed from Ze-Enna's face as she typed the following response, "You have no idea how much your message means to me! I'm so thrilled to know where I'm from! Thanks for responding! Thanks for welcoming me. I am looking forward to learning more and now a trip to the Motherland is even more necessary now that I really have a place to go and a bigger purpose! I'm so damn grateful! Again! I can't thank you enough! Love ya girl!"

Ze-Enna was overwhelmed that night. She was not alone.

Eight o-clock Saturday morning, we boarded five chartered buses at the hotel and headed to Abbeville, South Carolina. Seeing over 250 family members dressed in our light tan t-shirts was a sight to behold. Even the unity that the shirts exuded had astonished the travelers at the rest area near the Georgia-South Carolina state line where the buses stopped for a rest room break. With pride, Amelia took the time to explain to one of the travelers the history behind the reunion and why we were on our way to Abbeville. As if someone had told her that she had just won the Powerball lottery, the traveler commented, "That is amazing!" Amazing was an understatement.

Two hours and thirty minutes after departing Atlanta, we arrived in downtown Abbeville. Pleasant Barr's descendants had returned five years later, but this time we came back with the once-missing branch of the family tree – the Beckleys. After a scroll around the quaint downtown square, we gathered for an historic picture on the courthouse steps as passersby slowed down to marvel at the big gathering. That day, the temperature was a blazing ninety degrees. However, as we congregated, an overcast cloud suddenly appeared; it shielded the rays of the hot sun. Mother Nature provided much-welcomed shade and temporary coolness, as the temperature decreased by several degrees. We saw it as a sign from God and our ancestors. They were happy.

A visit to the Upper Long Cane Presbyterian Church and a visit to the Reid Place also adorned our meaningful itinerary. Moved by our presence and the purpose of our visit, the church's pastor, Dr. John Miller, anxiously found a seat on one of the buses and accompanied the family to the Old Zion Cemetery, the last stop of our tour. It was found to have been a very old cemetery possibly dating back to slavery. Overgrown with trees and bushes, and barely visible from Pecan Road, the cemetery contained a number of unmarked graves. Some of the remaining gravestones were of people who were born into slavery. Strangely, a few were more recent burials. Obviously, the cemetery had a long history since people had chosen to bury loved ones in an overgrown, wooded cemetery as late as 2003.

However, the cemetery was particularly special to us. It was situated on the land where Rev. William Barr's farm was once located. John Blythe and I were not certain if it had been a slave cemetery on the Barr farm. Nonetheless, we chose that cemetery to leave our mark in South Carolina – something that indicated what had taken place there on August 8, 2009, and something to recognize the existence of our patriarch, Lewis. Rebecca Barr's letter to her sister in February 1847 had indicated that he died in September 1846. Quite possibly, he may have been buried in that old cemetery, but, despite the uncertainty, we deemed it the best place for the granite commemorative marker. In my heart, I felt that Lewis's remains were somewhere out there, and this was our time to pay homage to him.

Amazingly, before our visit, the Abbeville-Greenwood, South Carolina Sons of Allen group, a male group affiliated with the African Methodist Episcopal Church (A.M.E.), had placed that cemetery on a special clean-up project – over a year prior to our visit. They were totally unaware of the possible significance of it and what would take place there over a year later. The ancestors had been working long before July 27, 2008, the day the planning team met for the first time. Upon learning about our plans, they stepped up their plans to clear more of the cemetery, so that it could be more visible from the road.

# City of Abbeville
## South Carolina

# Resolution

**Resolution No. 12-2009**

**A RESOLUTION TO EXTEND A WARM WELCOME TO THE DESCENDANTS
OF LEWIS AND FANNY BARR ON THEIR 150TH REUNION AND VISIT TO
ABBEVILLE, SOUTH CAROLINA**

**WHEREAS,** as Mayor of the City of Abbeville, South Carolina, I would like to congratulate and extend a warm welcome to the descendants of the Barr family on their visit "Back to Abbeville," and

**WHEREAS,** the event is being called **"The 150th Year Commemorative Reunion of the Descendants of Lewis and Fanny Barr."** Recent Genealogy research has revealed that the ancestors were from Abbeville, South Carolina, and were slaves on the plantation of Reverend Dr. William H. and Rebecca Reid Barr which was located three miles North of Abbeville, and

**WHEREAS,** beginning in 1859, various family members were transported to different states and areas without anyone knowing their whereabouts. In recent years members of the family have been located, and for the first time in one hundred and fifty years, after the family separated, a joyous reunion and celebration will be held beginning in Atlanta, Georgia and continuing in Abbeville, South Carolina. The family's motto is, we are **"Mending Family Ties, Rejoicing the Hearts of Our Ancestors,"** and

**WHEREAS,** the City of Abbeville is honored to have descendants of the Barr family visit Abbeville and the various points of interest during their stay, and

**WHEREAS,** we trust your trip to Abbeville will be a most pleasant experience, and we would like to extend an invitation to family members to come back to Abbeville and visit again.

**NOW, THEREFORE, BE IT RESOLVED,** that the Mayor and City Council of Abbeville, South Carolina on this 8th day of August 2009, extend their congratulations to the descendants of the Barr family and are proud to have them as a part of our Abbeville heritage.

Harold E. McNeill, Mayor
City of Abbeville, S.C.

August 8, 2009
Date

The leader of the group, James Finley, expressed, "What you all are doing is wonderful, beyond words. I never heard anything like this before." Thankfully, the group had been hard at work in the cemetery a week prior to our visit. Dressed in their black ties and pants and white shirts, they joined us in the dedication ceremony; the dedication was as equally meaningful to those eight men who probably had no blood connection to Lewis. Yet, there was a spiritual connection.

As the group gathered around the covered marker, eagerly anticipating the grand unveiling, we recited the following litany that Cousin Leroy had poignantly written and had led with Lewis's guidance:

Leader:  I stood on the banks of history and bore the pains of my people from past, present and future.

Audience:    You are our Ancestral Patriarch; speak to us; we hear you now.

Leader:  I heard the true stories from my ancestors as they told me about rich life in the Motherland Africa.

Audience:    You are our Ancestral Patriarch; speak to us; we hear you now.

Leader:  I heard the ancestors say that they were proud, noble, independent, and industrious people in the Motherland Africa.

Audience:    You are our Ancestral Patriarch; speak to us; we hear you now.

Leader:  I heard the ancestors say that they were snatched from their relatives, placed in chains, marched to dungeons, placed in small dehumanizing cells for months at a time, marched through a door of no return, loaded on slave ships, placed in more small dehumanizing cells, crossed the rolling seas, traveled thousands of miles, dispersed to foreign lands, and sold like cattle on auction blocks.

Audience:   You are our Ancestral Patriarch; we feel your pains; speak to us; we hear you now.

Leader:   I was born in this foreign land, worked all my life on a plantation, experienced the bitter chastening rods, married Fanny, and raised strong children under severe adverse circumstances.

Audience:   You are our Ancestral Patriarch; we are the children of your great-grandchildren, your great-great-grandchildren, and your great-great-great-grandchildren; we benefited from your severe suffering and great sacrifices; speak to us; we hear you now.

Leader:   God brought us through our gloomy past, weary years, and silent tears.

Audience:   You are our Ancestral Patriarch; speak to us; we hear you now.

Leader:   At last, you have found Abbeville and my resting place. You are my descendants. Though split by unfavorable conditions that were not decided by you nor me, you have found each other. Stay together. I prayed for you. I am proud of you.

Audience:  You are our Ancestral Patriarch; we came from North, East, South, and West to visit your resting place; we salute your life by laying a tombstone at your head to remind you of your two major branches of Beckleys and Reeds; continue to speak to us throughout the ages; we hear you now.

Leader:  Sing me a Zion song and let my soul rest in peace.

Representatives from the African-American-owned Richie's Funeral Home lifted the Kente cloth veil from the beautiful commemorative marker. The planning team had only seen its design on paper. I could not fight the tears. At that very moment, I felt as if I was burying someone I had known personally for years, someone who had a great influence on my life. Lewis had died 126 years before his great-great-granddaughter birthed me into the world. Yet, that day, I felt his love. I felt his pain and sufferings. I felt his happiness. Undoubtedly, I felt his presence. He was my ancestor, and the ancestor of all of us, and at that moment, I felt an unbelievably strong bond to him – someone who I had only known by name on a slave inventory and on a letter written by his slave mistress. I felt connected.

Departing Abbeville on Saturday evening headed back to Atlanta, I now had that feeling of completion that I was seeking. The next morning, *The Index-Journal*, the main newspaper for the Abbeville-Greenwood area, headlined us on their front page with the heading, "More than 230 return to their roots in Abbeville." We had walked where our ancestors walked. More importantly, we had also done something that Cannon Beckley's great-great-grandson, Preston Beckley III, conveyed to the family at our Sunday morning farewell breakfast at the Westin. Having heard the following phrase recited at weddings, he realized that the words were appropriately fitting for the weekend we had just experienced: "What God has joined together, the Reeds and the Beckleys, let no man put asunder."

*252 family members boarding five chartered buses in Atlanta to journey to Abbeville, South Carolina, August 8, 2009*

*The family toured downtown Abbeville, South Carolina, August 8, 2009*

*The family gathered inside Upper Long Cane Presbyterian Church, Abbeville, South Carolina, August 8, 2009*

The family visited the Session House at Upper Long Cane Presbyterian Church. After professing their Faith in the Session House, the slaves, who were owned by members of the church, attended the services where they sat in slave galleries.

Dedication of a marker for the family ancestor, Lewis, that was placed in an old slave cemetery, believed to be on land where the Barr farm was located. Lewis died somewhere in the vicinity in September 1846.

Excited about the occasion, the Abbeville-Greenwood, South Carolina Sons of Allen Male Group participated in the dedication ceremony by singing a song. They worked diligently to clear the cemetery for the ceremony.

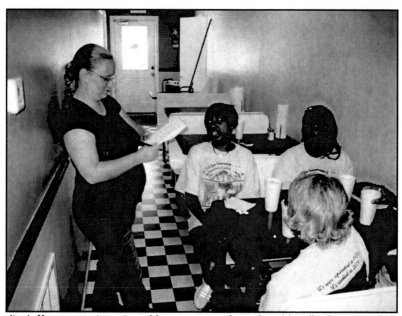

Amelia Jefferson was interviewed by a reporter from the Abbeville-Greenwood, South Carolina newspaper, Index-Journal, which printed a feature article about the event.

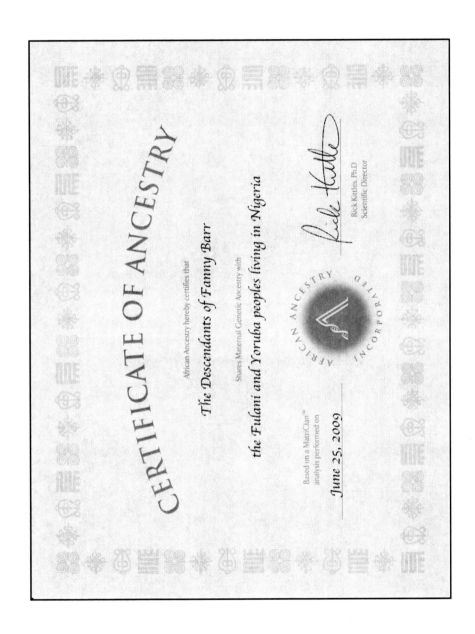

*The Planning Committee: left to right, Melvin J. Collier, Dr. Leroy Frazier, Clara Hunter King, Ouida Howard, Denise Harrington, Jerilyn Beckley, and Frank Turpin. Not pictured: Amelia Jefferson and Vikki Jenkins*

*Melvin J. Collier and Mayor Harold McNeill, City of Abbeville*

# Epilogue

*O*n July 2, 2011, during the 54th Annual Beckley Family Reunion, descendants of Fanny Barr's children, Sue and Pleasant, gathered at the College Hill Cemetery just east of Pontotoc, Mississippi to dedicate a commemorative marker in her honor. One was placed and dedicated in Abbeville, South Carolina for her husband Lewis in 2009, during the 150th Year Commemorative Reunion; an almost identical marker was designed for Fanny.

Fanny lived under the dark cloud of chattel slavery in three states – Virginia, South Carolina, and Mississippi. She had involuntarily traveled thousands of miles, as her fate had been determined by others. She could not say, "No, I don't want to go" or "Please don't take me there." That was not up to her. I can only imagine the struggles that she endured during her life as a slave. I am certain that some things are not even imaginable at all; they were too inhumane to comprehend.

Although I currently lack any concrete details about her early life, I mentally picture a young girl, who was probably under the comfort of her mother and father, my unidentified great-great-great-great-grandparents, and perhaps her Nigeria-born maternal grandmother – also unidentified – on a tobacco plantation in Virginia. Then, one day her enslaver decided that she was old enough to sell to a slave trader for a very good price, a trader who sold black bodies to planters in the Deep South. Many Virginia slaves were always under the threat of being "sold down South" where cotton had become the leading cash crop and more free labor was essential. In my mind, I picture this trader transporting a coffle of slaves – adults and children – through Virginia and North Carolina until he reached upstate South Carolina. I picture Rev. William H. Barr negotiating a price for young and tired Fanny on the town square in Abbeville. My heart becomes heavy, as this mental picture probably does not deviate too far from the actual events of Fanny's early life – events that I hope to positively glean more factual information in the future.

Unlike many slaves who were also born during the last decade of the eighteenth century, Fanny was able to taste sweet freedom for the last twenty or so years of her long life. While her son, Glasgow, had been forced to remain in Abbeville, South Carolina and her son, Pleasant, had been sold to James Giles, who took him to Ripley, Mississippi, Fanny was able to live among her daughter Sue's children and grandchildren in Pontotoc County, Mississippi during those sweet years of freedom. When the 1880 census-taker visited Rev. Jacob Beckley's home on July 2nd of that year to record the names, ages, birthplaces, and other data of everyone in that household, he probably found Jacob's elderly grandmother rocking comfortably in her rocking chair. Fanny was blind, as noted in the census, but she was at peace. She was a free woman; slavery had been long gone.

Rest in peace, Grandma Fanny Barr. You are not forgotten.

# Acknowledgments

$\mathcal{I}$ am forever indebted to my family for their rich oral accounts of our family's history. Their stories were invaluable, and without it, this journey into Grandpa Bill Reed's history would have been met with many brick walls. I thank God for their profound wisdom, their willingness to share, and for always being very enthusiastic to talk about the history of our family. These special people are the late Isaac Deberry Sr., the late Rev. John Deberry Sr., the late Enos Reed, the late Steve Reed, Armentha Reed Puryear, Robert E. Puryear, Sarah Deberry Smith, Eartha Reed Campbell, Angela Walton-Raji, John W. Reed Sr., Willie M. Frazier, and Rev. H. L. Reed.

Many thanks to my loving and supportive parents, Jimmie & Versia Reed Collier, my beautiful sisters, LaVonda Hart and Iva Gaston, my smart niece Jori, and my smart nephews, Jordan, Jerron, Jeremiah, Charles Jr., and Xavier, for their love and support. A special thanks is extended to my wonderful mother for telling me, with love, pride, and enthusiasm, about her unforgettable childhood years growing up on the Old Home Place in Tate County, Mississippi. Although her father Simpson Reed died before I was born, our many conversations about my grandfather enabled me to know the type of wonderful husband he was to my grandmother, a wonderful father he was to my mother and her siblings, and a wonderful uncle to many nieces and nephews. This made me very proud to be a Reed.

A special thanks to my many cousins for their support and enthusiasm. I am blessed to have loving cousins like Dr. Leroy Frazier, Wallace Reed, Devonia Morrow, Vernice Hibbler, Ruthie Clark, Betty Williams, Albertina Reed, Belinda Hicks, Orien Nix, Amelia Jefferson, Ouida Howard, Vikki Jenkins, James A. Reed, Clara King, Claiborne Reed, Dr. Rhonda Reed, Angela Hudson, Rosalind Reed, Bettina Reed, Kelvin Reed, Cynthia Lee, Caronde Puryear, Judy Williams, Kenneth Johnson, Jerilyn Beckley, Frank Turpin, Denise Harrington, Monica Campbell, Charlotte Bandele, Kwame Bandele, Gabriel Reed, John Reed Jr., Derrick Powell, Lisa Powell, Renata Frazier, Dr. Rosie Milligan, Andrea Wright, Nancy Payne, Raime Reed, Kristina Hayes, Vivian Hayes, Machelle Easley, Cora Collins, Doris Bradshaw, Roger W. Reed Jr., **to name a few**. The list is very large, and I thank God for being part of a great extended family who values family connections.

Many thanks go to the staff at the Mississippi Department of Archives and History, the Memphis-Shelby County Library, the South Carolina Department of Archives and History, John Blythe and Rose-Marie Williams of the Abbeville County Historical Society, and Brent Grisham of the Ripley Public Library for their invaluable assistance. Many thanks also go to the late Wayne Reid, Michael Barr, Bob Thompson, and the late Frederick Spight. If I miss anyone, please charge it to my head and not my heart. Your involvement was not forgotten and is greatly appreciated.

# Endnotes

## Introduction

[1] Harriet A. Jacobs, *Incidents in the Life of a Slave Girl* (Cambridge: Harvard University Press, 1987), 16.

## Chapter 1

[1] Stewart E. Tolnay and E.M. Beck, *A Festival of Violence, An Analysis of Southern Lynching, 1882-1930* (Urbana and Chicago, IL: University of Illinois, 1995), 17.

[2] Niara Sudarkasa, "Interpreting the African Heritage in Afro-American Family Organization", in Harriette Pipes McAdoo, ed. *Black Families* (Beverly Hills: SAGE, 1981), 18.

[3] Ione D. Vargus, *More Than a Picnic: African-American Family Reunion*, The Emory Center for Myth and Ritual in American Life, Working Paper No. 21, 2002.

[4] Robert E. Puryear, 1992 Reed-Puryear Family Reunion Book (unpublished), 1.

[5] Works Project Administration, Federal Writers Project, *Slave Narratives: A Folk History of Slavery in the United States from Interviews with Former Slaves,* the narrative of Levi Ashley, Ancestry.com, http://www.ancestry.com, accessed 07 September 2009.

[6] Angela Y. Walton-Raji, e-mail message to Melvin J. Collier, April 30, 1994.

# Chapter 3

[1] Angela Y. Walton-Raji, e-mail message to Melvin J. Collier, March 25, 1996.

[2] Works Project Administration, Federal Writers Project, *Slave Narratives: A Folk History of Slavery in the United States from Interviews with Former Slaves,* the narrative of Mandy Jones, Ancestry.com, http://www.ancestry.com, accessed 09 September 2009.

[3] Works Project Administration, Federal Writers Project, *Slave Narratives: A Folk History of Slavery in the United States from Interviews with Former Slaves,* the narrative of Delia Garlie, Ancestry.com, http://www.ancestry.com, accessed 08 September 2009.

[4] Maris Vinovskis, *Toward a Social History of the American Civil War: Exploratory Essays* (Cambridge, Cambridge University Press, 1990), 172.

[5] Amanda Young, widow's pension file, deposition 2, in the case of Amanda Young, claim no. 1049438, The National Archives, Washington, D.C.

[6] Wyatt Carter, widow's pension file, deposition 3, in the case of Amanda Young, claim no. 1049438, The National Archives, Washington, D.C.

[7] Frances Nelson, widow's pension file, deposition 7, in the case of Amanda Young, claim no. 1049438, The National Archives, Washington, D.C.

[8] Sam Edgerton, widow's pension file, deposition 4, in the case of Amanda Young, claim no. 1049438, The National Archives, Washington, D.C.

[9] Michael Barr, e-mail message to Melvin J. Collier, February 21, 1998.

[10] *The Heritage of Tippah County, Mississippi* (Tippah County Historical Society, 1991).

[11] Frederick L. Spight (deceased), letter to Melvin J. Collier, March 19, 1998.

[12] *The Heritage of Tippah County, Mississippi* (Tippah County Historical Society, 1991).

# Chapter 4

[1] Wayne Alexander Reid (deceased), letter to Melvin J. Collier, May 7, 1998.

[2] James G. Leyburn, *The Scotch-Irish, A Social History* (Chapel Hill: The University of North Carolina Press, 1962).

[3] Roger Daniels, *Coming to America: A History of Immigration and Ethnicity in American Life,* 2nd ed. (New York: Harper Perennial, 2002), 144.

[4] Daniel C. Littlefield, *Rice and Slaves: Ethnicity and the Slave Trade in Colonial South Carolina* (Chicago: University of Illinois Press, 1981), 116.

[5] Gwendolyn Midlo Hall, *Slavery and African Ethnicities in the Americas: Restoring the Links* (Chapel Hill: University of North Carolina Press, 2005), 94.

[6] Ibid., 179.

[7] Philip D. Morgan, *Slave Counterpoint: Black Culture in the Eighteenth-Century Chesapeake and Low-Country* (Chapel Hill: University of North Carolina Press, 1998), 95.

[8] Wayne Reid, *The 1860 Diary of Lemuel Reid, an Abbeville District, South Carolina Planter* (Self-published, 1994), 9.

[9] Carl J. Schneider and Dorothy Schneider, *An Eyewitness History of Slavery in America* (New York: Checkmark Books, 2001), 82.

[10] Herbert J. Foster, "African Patterns in the Afro-American Family," *Journal of Black Studies* 14, no. 2 (1983): 218.

[11] Wayne Alexander Reid, *The 1860 Diary of Lemuel Reid, an Abbeville District, South Carolina Planter* (Self-published, 1994), 13.

[12] John Blassingame, *The Slave Community: Plantation Life in the Antebellum South* (New York: Oxford University Press, 1972), 155.

[13] Ibid.

[14] Frederick Law Olmsted, *The Cotton Kingdom* (New York: De Capo Press, Inc., 1953), 432.

[15] Wayne Alexander Reid, *The 1861, January 1862, and January 1864 Diaries of Lemuel Reid, an Abbeville District, South Carolina Planter and Confederate Army Officer* (Self-published, 2000), 44.

[16] Kai Wright, *Soldiers of Freedom, An Illustration History of African Americans in the Armed Forces* (New York: Black Dog & Leventhal, 2002), 84.

17 Wayne Alexander Reid, *The 1861, January 1862, and January 1864 Diaries of Lemuel Reid, an Abbeville District, South Carolina Planter and Confederate Army Officer* (Self-published, 2000), 2.

18 Dorothy Spruill Redford, *Somerset Homecoming, Recovering a Lost Heritage* (Chapel Hill: University of North Carolina Press, 2000), 146.

# Chapter 5

1 Works Project Administration, Federal Writers Project, *Slave Narratives: A Folk History of Slavery in the United States from Interviews with Former Slaves,* the narrative of William Anderson, Ancestry.com, http://www.ancestry.com, accessed 19 September 2009.

2 Works Project Administration, Federal Writers Project, *Slave Narratives: A Folk History of Slavery in the United States from Interviews with Former Slaves,* the narrative of Lewis Brown, Ancestry.com, http://www.ancestry.com, accessed 19 September 2009.

3 Dee Parmer Woodtor, *Finding A Place Called Home, A Guide to African-American Genealogy and Historical Identity* (New York: Random House, 1999), 299-300.

4 Carl J. Schneider and Dorothy Schneider, *An Eyewitness History of Slavery in America* (NewYork: Checkmark Books, 2001), 116.

5 Frances Anne Kemble, *Journal of a Residence on a Georgian Plantation in 1838-1839* (New York: Alfred A. Knopf, 1961), 312.

# Chapter 7

1 Ira Berlin & Leslie S. Rowland, ed., *Families & Freedom: A Documentary History of African-American Kinship in the Civil War Era* (New York: The New Press, 1997), 17.

[2] John Baker, Jr., *The Washington of Wessyngton Plantation, Stories of my Family's Journey to Freedom* (New York: Atria Books, 2009), 225.

[3] Franklin L. Riley, *Publications of the Mississippi Historical Society* (Oxford: University of Mississippi, 1910), 257.

[4] Ibid.

[5]

http://homepage.mac.com/bfthompson/miller_reid_families/Milreidfa m/ps04_387.htm, assessed 04 October 2009.

[6] University of Mississippi, *Catalogue of the officers and students of the University of Mississippi at Oxford, Mississippi* (Jackson: Clarion Stream Publishing House, 1880), no page number listed.

# Chapter 8

[1] John Blythe, e-mail message to Melvin J. Collier, May 11, 2004.

[2] A. James Reichley, *Faith in Politics* (Washington, DC: The Brookings Institution, 2002), 180.

[3] James H. Smylie, *A Brief History of the Presbyterians* (Louisville, KY, Geneva Press, 1996), 78.

[4] William B. Sprague, *Annals of the American Pulpit; Commemorative Notices of Distinguished American Clergymen of Various Denominations, Volume IV* (New York: Robert Carter and Brothers, 1860), 385-387.

[5] Maulana Karenga, "Black Religion," in *African-American Religious Studies* by G. S. Wilmore (Durham: Duke University Press, 1998).

[6] Harriet A. Jacobs, *Incidents in the Life of a Slave Girl* (Cambridge: Harvard University Press, 1987), 69.

[7] *Memorial Volume of the Semi-Centennial of the Theological Seminary at Columbia, South Carolina* (Columbia, SC: Presbyterian Publishing House, 1884), 16.

[8] Stevenson, Pearl M., *Keeping the Faith: A History of Upper Long Cane Presbyterian Church* (Greenwood, SC, Drinkard Publishing, 1976), 13-18.

[9] Ibid, 17.

[10] Albert J. Raboteau, *Slave Religion: the "Invisible Institution" in the Antebellum South* (New York: Oxford University Press, 1978), 243.

[11] Works Project Administration, Federal Writers Project, *Slave Narratives: A Folk History of Slavery in the United States from Interviews with Former Slaves,* the narrative of Hannah Austin, Ancestry.com, http://www.ancestry.com, accessed 17 October 2009.

[12] Works Project Administration, Federal Writers Project, *Slave Narratives: A Folk History of Slavery in the United States from Interviews with Former Slaves,* the narrative of Mingo White, Ancestry.com, http://www.ancestry.com, accessed 06 October 2009.

[13] Works Project Administration, Federal Writers Project, *Slave Narratives: A Folk History of Slavery in the United States from Interviews with Former Slaves,* the narrative of Anna Morgan, Ancestry.com, http://www.ancestry.com, accessed 06 October 2009.

[14] Works Project Administration, Federal Writers Project, *Slave Narratives: A Folk History of Slavery in the United States from Interviews with Former Slaves,* the narrative of Mary Ella Grandberry, Ancestry.com, http://www.ancestry.com, accessed 17 October 2009.

[15] Works Project Administration, Federal Writers Project, *Slave Narratives: A Folk History of Slavery in the United States from Interviews*

with *Former Slaves,* the narrative of Minerva Grubbs, Ancestry.com, http://www.ancestry.com, accessed 06 October 2009.

[16] John W. Blassingame, ed., *Slave Testimony: Two Centuries of Letters, Speeches, Interviews, and Autobiographies* (Baton Rouge: Louisiana State University Press, 1977), 4.

# Chapter 9

[1] Bob Thompson, e-mail message to Melvin J. Collier, July 4, 2004.

[2] Letter transcribed by Bob Thompson.

[3] Letter transcribed by Bob Thompson.

[4] Letter transcribed by Bob Thompson.

[5] John Blassingame, *The Slave Community: Plantation Life in the Antebellum South* (New York: Oxford University Press, 1972), 45.

# Chapter 10

[1] Kenneth L. Waters, Sr., *Afrocentric Sermons: The Beauty of Blackness in the Bible* (Valley Forge, PA: Judson Press, 1993), 37.

[2] Vincent Harding, *There Is a River: The Black Struggle for Freedom in America* (New York: Harcourt Brace and Company, 1981), 27.

[3] Hazel Neat, letter to Florence Bolden, April 9, 1977.

[4] Doris Posey, *Black Confederate Pension Records, A controversial resource for African American researchers,* in <u>The Epoch Times</u>, Feb. 1, 2008.

[5] Callie B. Young, ed., *From These Hills, A History of Pontotoc County* (Mantachie, MS: Mantachie Printing, 1993), 184.

# Chapter 11

[1] Doria Johnson, "The Lynching of Anthony Crawford," http://www.ccharity.com/content/lynching-anthony-crawford, accessed on 06 October 2009.

[2] Ibid.

[3] Ibid.

[4] Shelley Reid, e-mail message to Melvin J. Collier, July 18, 2004.

[5] Catherine Willis, e-mail message to Reed-Puryear Family Yahoo Group, July 21, 2004.

# Chapter 12

[1] Melvin J. Collier, e-mail message to the Beckley Family yahoo group, July 23, 2006.

[2] Kenneth L. Johnson, e-mail message to the Beckley Family yahoo group, July 23, 2006.

[3] Michael A. Gomez, *Exchanging Our Country Marks: The Transformation of African Identities in the Colonial and Antebellum South* (Chapel Hill: University of North Carolina Press, 1998), 136.

# Notes

_____

_____

_____

_____

_____

_____

_____

_____

_____

_____

_____

_____

_____

_____

_____

_____

# Index

## 1 - 100

59th Regiment Infantry, 83
150th Year Commemorative
    Reunion, 194, 213
The 1820 Census of Abbeville
    County, South Carolina, 103
The 1830 Census of Abbeville
    County, South Carolina, 103
1860 agricultural census, 72
The 1860 Diary of Lemuel Reid, an
    Abbeville District, South Carolina
    Planter, 66, 68
1880 U. S. Federal Census, 33, 43, 92

## A

Abbeville County, 50-52, 65, 72, 75,
    86, 88, 97, 100, 103, 112, 120,
    135, 159, 168, 170-172, 174
Abbeville County Penal Farm, 168
Abbeville District, 66-71, 159
Abbeville Historical Society, 119,
    170, 172
Abram (slave), 73, 129, 141
Africa, 6, 9, 15, 26, 70, 93, 132, 141,
    157-158, 197-198, 204
African Ancestry, Inc., 199
African population, 69-70

African traditional religions, 124
African-American Lives, 156
Africanity, 157, 159
AfriGeneas.com, 64, 154, 193
Akan, 9
Alabama, 4, 29, 46, 105, 110, 115-116,
    122, 124, 132
Alexander, Gladys, 33
Alfred (slave), 140, 167-168
Alice (slave), 140
America Online, 21-22, 50
American Revolution, 70
Amite County, Mississippi, 18
Anderson, William, 91
Angola, 9, 197-199
Angola-Congo Africans, 198
Annapolis, Maryland, 1
Arkansas, 4, 91, 110, 169
Aron (slave), 73-74
Ashley, Levi, 18
Association of Angolans in Georgia
    (ASSANGA), 197
Athens, Georgia, 121
Atlanta, Georgia, 10-11, 151, 162-163,
    169, 181-182, 185-188, 192-195,
    200, 206-207
Atlanta Beckley Club, 187-188, 192
Atlantic Ocean, 158, 198

Auburn Avenue Research Library, 186
Augusta County, Virginia, 67
Austin, Hannah, 131

# B

Baker, John, 107
Bandele, Kwame, 13
baptisms, 119, 129
Barr, Elijah, 22, 42-43, 47
Barr, Fannie, 111
Barr, Fanny or "Fanny", 72-73, 90-93, 100-101, 103-104, 109, 111-113, 117-119, 126-128, 130, 137-139, 141, 152, 154, 161, 165, 187, 189-192, 194, 196-197, 199, 205, 213-214
Barr farm, 62, 81, 91-93, 95-96, 99-103, 117, 138-139, 150, 163, 179-180, 201, 209
Barr, George, 97
Barr, Glasgow, 130, 167-168
Barr Hall, 116
Barr, Hugh Alexander, 115-117
Barr, Isabella, 111, 113, 152, 161
Barr, Margaret, 52, 77, 95, 100-101, 126
Barr, Michael, 50, 87
Barr, Oliver, 97
Barr, Pleasant (Pleas), 22-23, 41-50, 53-54, 56-58, 60-62, 87-88, 100, 109, 130, 134, 143, 147, 149-150, 160, 163, 184, 190-191, 193, 195, 197, 200
Barr, Rebecca Reid, 51-52, 71, 76, 87-88, 92, 96-97, 100, 103, 115, 135-136, 138, 141, 155, 181, 201
Barr, Samuel McCorkle, 95
Barr, Sawney, 108
Barr, William, 51-52, 76-77, 96-97, 101, 103, 108-109, 111-112, 115, 117-118, 126-127, 130, 139, 144, 149, 154, 161-162, 177, 179, 201

Barr, William H. (Rev.), 51, 71, 87-90, 100, 103, 115, 117, 119, 121, 177, 189, 201, 214
Barrtown, Mississippi, 153
Baskin, Betsey, 137
Battle of Manassas, 162
Battle of Mechanicsville, Virginia, 85
Beckley, Edmond, 112, 144, 160-162, 165
Beckley, Cannon, 112, 144, 146-147, 151, 163, 165-166, 190, 199, 206
Beckley, Clay or Henry Clay, 111-113, 117-118, 144, 150, 152-153, 155, 165
Beckley, David, 147, 165-166
Beckley, Estelle, 199
Beckley Family Clubs, 150
Beckley Family Reunion, 151, 162, 164-165, 169, 187-189, 191, 213
Beckley Five, 146, 163-165
Beckley, Hattie, 149, 199
Beckley, Jacob, 111-112, 114, 117, 154, 156, 164-165, 168, 214
Beckley, Jacob (Rev.), 114, 127, 130, 144, 146, 163-165, 214
Beckley, Jerilyn, 193, 212
Beckley, John, 115
Beckley, Lemuel "Lem", 152
Beckley, Lewis, 112, 114, 117, 144-145, 149, 165
Beckley, Louvenia, 144, 150, 199
Beckley, Maurice, 163-164
Beckley, Patsy, 116
Beckley, Preston III, 206
Beckley, Preston IV, 151
Beckley, Ruby, 163
Beckley, Sue Barr, 114, 117, 190-191, 195, 199
Beckley, Susie, 114, 116
Bella (slave), 90, 94, 100-102, 104-105, 110-111, 113, 129
Benton Harbor, Michigan, 8
Beulah Baptist Church, 3, 7-8, 30-31, 37, 176

# Index

Bible, 3, 15, 123, 125, 131
Bickley, John, 159
Bixby, Steven, 170
Black History Month, 2
Black, Lucy, 144
Bloody Sunday, 115
Blythe, John, 119, 170, 174, 179, 201
Bobo, Eli, 15
Bobo, John Ella Reed, 2, 7, 15, 17
Bolden, Florence, 160
Bowen, Bobby, 179
Bowie, Alexander, 122
Bowie, Nancy J., 74, 136
Brady, Samuel, 156
Brame, Martha Beckley, 152
Branch, William Tully, 179
Bronson, Lewis, 91
Brooks, Martha, 144

## C

Campbell, Eartha (Aunt Eartha), 2, 5, 7, 12, 16, 24, 26, 54, 147, 197
Canton, Mississippi, 6-7, 10, 13
Capoeira Angola, 197
Carr, Alfred, 156
Carry (slave), 140
Carter, Wyatt, 47
Carthage, Mississippi, 157
Cater, Edwin, 126
Charleston, South Carolina, 69-70, 179, 198
Charleston earthquake, 179
chattel slavery, 1, 90, 95, 121, 124, 159, 189, 213
Cherokee Indians, 69
Chicago, Illinois, 7, 10, 150, 171, 186, 190-191, 195
Chicago Beckley Club, 190-191
Chickasaw County, Mississippi, 91
Christianity, 124-125, 131
church minutes, 119, 126, 164
church records, 55-56, 119-120, 132, 135, 167
Civil Engineering, 20

Civil Rights, 115
Civil War, 12, 18, 22, 32, 40, 42, 45-46, 49, 61, 66, 72, 76, 83, 87, 108-109, 116-117, 150, 153-154, 161, 180, 184
Clark Atlanta University, 186, 192
Clemson, 65-66
Cleveland, Ohio, 151
Cobb, Everjean Brame, 152
Cobb, Thomas Black, 107
Cole, W. R., 53
College Hill, 153, 155, 163, 166, 213
Collier, Versia, 24
Como, Mississippi, 3, 7, 37
Confederate Army, 161
contraband camps, 49
cotton, 16, 65-66, 74, 76, 79-84, 133, 171, 214
Crawford, Anthony, 171

## D

DNA, 156, 197-199
Danner, Edward, 83
Davis, John Hector, 3
Davis, Lucy Milam, 53
death certificate, 40-42, 44, 99, 104, 114, 117, 164, 168
Deberry, Essie Kay, 33
Deberry, Isaac (Cousin Ike), 25-35, 40, 42, 44-45, 52, 72-73, 81-83, 85, 92-95, 99, 102, 104, 146, 163, 167-170, 174-177, 180, 184, 190
Deberry, John, 45
Deberry, Martha Jane, 15, 24-26
Deberry, Ollie, 15
DeSoto County, Mississippi, 19, 21, 27
diary, 65-66, 72-73, 78, 80-82
Dillard, Jane, 144
Dropshot (slave), 73-74
Dusenberry, Reid, 66

# E

Easley, Machelle Reed, 187
Edgerton, Sam, 48, 60-61
education, 4, 54, 57, 64, 122
Egypt, 131, 157
Elbert (slave), 51, 77, 90, 94, 100-101
Emancipation, 43, 86
Emancipation Proclamation, 49, 83
England, 69
Erskine, 74
estate appraisers, 91, 93, 97
estate records, 87-88

# F

Facebook, 199
famine, 67
Fernandes, Lucia, 197
Finley, James, 204
Fitzpatrick, Sarah, 132
Fourteenth Amendment, 109
Franklin College, 121
Franklin, Lennie, 144
Frazier, Leroy (Cousin Leroy), 10, 33-
    34, 57, 60, 62, 147-148, 163-166,
    169, 174-175, 185, 193, 195, 204,
    212
Freedmen Bureau, 107
funeral rites, 141

# G

Gambia, 1
Garlie, Delia, 46
Gates, Henry Louis, 156
Geeter High School, 54
General Order 143, 83
Ghana, 9, 157
Giles, James, 49-50, 88, 117, 139, 214
Giles, John H., 49
Giles, Frances, 49
Gilmore, Rose Ann, 137
Glasgo (slave), 73

Grand Matriarch of the Beckley
    Family, 148
Grandberry, Mary Ella, 132
Gray, Myrtle, 59
Great Awakening, 125
Great Depression, 3, 76
Greater Abbeville Chamber of
    Commerce, 173
Green Hill Plantation, 142
Green, John, 15
griot, 25, 27
Grubbs, Minerva, 132

# H

Haley, Alex, 1
Hall, Gwendolyn Midlo, 70
Harmony Church, Mississippi, 127-
    128
Harrington, Denise, 193, 212
Harriot, Jannie, 173
The Heritage of Tate County,
    Mississippi, 52
The Heritage of Tippah County,
    Mississippi, 53
Hibbler, James, 34
Holly Springs, 54, 114, 130, 144, 153
Homecoming Day, 7-8
Hope, Leighton, 46
Howard, Bertha, 2
Howard, Ouida, 151-153, 163, 187,
    192, 196-197, 212
Howland, Ruth, 172, 181
Hoyt, Thomas A., 131
Hoyt, Rev. J. A., 130
Hunter, Louvenia, 27
Hunter, Simon, 31
Hunters Chapel Church, 31
Hutchinson, Tommy Lynn, 199

# I

Illinois, 8, 10, 150, 169, 171, 194
Index-Journal, 206, 210
Israel (slave), 73-74, 82, 129

**J**

Jacobs, Harriet, 125
Jefferson, Amelia, 187, 200, 210, 212
Jefferson County, Mississippi, 71
Jefferson, Jane, 170
Jefferson, Thomas, 155
Jenkins, Vikki, 160-161, 163, 193, 212
Jenkins, Ze-Enna, 199
Jobe (slave), 73
Johnson, Celia, 156
Johnson, Doria Dee, 171
Johnson, James, 59
Johnson, Kenneth, 190
Jones, Mandy, 43
Jude (slave), 137

**K**

Kentucky Fried Chicken, 62
King, Clara, 193
King, Martin Luther, 167, 182
kinship network, 9
Kittles, Rick, 199
Klu Klux Klan, 109
Knight, Gladys, 176
Knox, Carolyn, 63
Kunta Kinte, 1
Kyle, James, 138, 140

**L**

Lafayette County, Mississippi, 114-117, 126, 155
Lancaster County, Pennsylvania, 67
Lang, Jeffrey, 177
Leake County, Mississippi, 39, 157
Lee, Edward, 182
Lee County, Iowa, 71
Lee, Cunningham, 181
Lee, Mary Reed, 15
Lee, Susie Reid, 181
Lesley, David, 136, 140
Lesley, John W., 154
Lesley, William, 130

Leslie, A. E., 74, 77
Leslie, J. J., 77
Lesly, James, 140
Letty (slave), 140
Lewis, 55, 73, 90-93, 101, 103, 113, 118-119, 130, 138, 141, 149-150, 152-153, 155, 165, 187, 189-192, 194, 196-199, 201, 204, 206, 209, 213
Lincoln, Abraham, 49
Livingstone, J. Fraser, 130
London (slave), 130, 133
Long Cane Creek, 69
Long Cane Society, 69
Looxahoma, 8, 16, 20, 40
Louisa County, Virginia, 159
Louisiana, 4
Lowndnesville, South Carolina, 169
Luther (slave), 51, 90, 94, 101, 155, 167, 182
Lyles, Sam, 29
lynching, 3-4, 171-172

**M**

Mali, 157
Mariah (slave), 51, 77, 90, 94, 100-102, 104-105, 180
Marinda (slave), 96, 100-101, 103-104, 110, 113, 118, 126-128
Marshall County, Mississippi, 114
Martin, Junius, 74
Martin, Stark, 74
Maryland, 1, 43, 169, 199
Mbundu, 9, 198
McCoy, Abraham, 53
McCoy, Elijah, 91
McCoy, Dr. Lee Marcus, 53-54, 147
McKee, Fanny, 93, 104
McKee, Frank, 93
McNeill, Harold, 174, 178, 212
Means, Ben, 77
Means, James, 74

Memphis, Tennessee, 10, 15, 22, 33, 42, 47-48, 50, 52, 54, 60, 146, 148-150, 185-186
Memphis Public Library, 50, 52
Michigan, 7-8, 191
Middle Passage, 198
Miller, Ebenezer, 71
Miller, John, 201
Miller, Joseph, 71
Milwaukee, Wisconsin, 150, 152
miscegenation, 155
Mississippi Beckley Club, 163
Mississippi death index, 40
Mississippi Department of Archives and History (MDAH), 13, 19, 27, 40, 114
Mississippi Historical Society, 108
Mississippi State University, 20
Montgomery, Alabama, 46
Morgan, Anna, 132
Motherland, 2, 200, 204
mulatto, 102, 104, 112, 127, 149, 154-157

**N**

naming practice, 26
Nashville, Tennessee, 10-11, 192
Natchez, Mississippi, 81
National Archives, 46, 110
Neat, Hazel, 160
Ned (slave), 73
Negro spiritual, 34, 177
Nelson, Frances, 47
New York City, 76
Nigeria, 9, 199-200, 214
Norman (slave), 140

**O**

Obama, Barack Hussein, 194
O'Hara, Scarlett, 67
Ohio, 8, 151
Old Ben (slave), 73

Old Home Place, 8-10, 14-17, 19-20, 25, 33, 36, 45, 118, 177
Old Testament, 131
Old Zion Cemetery, 201
Olmstead, Frederick, 81
Operation Impact, 173
Orlando, Florida, 150
Ouzts, Donnie, 170
Oxford, Mississippi, 114-116, 144

**P**

Panola County, Mississippi, 7, 15, 18-19, 29, 31, 82, 104, 180
Partee, Claimus, 15
Partee, Dempsey, 15
Partee, Druella, 15
Partee, Jack, 15
Partee, Square, 15, 30
Pate, Derrick, 23
Pecan Road, 179, 201
Penn Center, 173
Pensacola, Florida, 10-11, 187
pension, 42, 46, 48, 55, 161
Perrin, T. C., 130
Person, Addie, 14
Pettus, Edmund, 115
Pettus, William S., 115
Philadelphia, Pennsylvania, 121
pneumonia, 28, 42
Pontotoc County, Mississippi, 71, 76-77, 95, 97, 108-109, 111-112, 114, 117-118, 126-127, 139, 144-145, 147, 150-151, 154-155, 161-163, 166, 190, 214
Pontotoc Minute Men, 162
Port Royal, South Carolina, 133
Pratcher, Aristarcus, 15
Pratt, David, 31
Pratt, Mary, 31, 193
Presbyterian General Assembly, 122
Presbyterians, 69, 121-122
*Press and Banner*, 181
Pryor, Anderson, 53

Puryear, Armentha Reed, 7-8, 10, 12, 33, 36, 45, 174, 178
Puryear, Edward, 10
Puryear, Julie, 10
Puryear, Lucious, 8
Puryear, Robert (Cousin Bob), 8, 12, 17, 19, 38

**R**

Ray, Lilly, 172
Reconstruction, 3, 12, 57, 108-109
Redford, Dorothy Spruill, 85
Reed, Bettina, 186
Reed, Bill, 2, 6, 12, 18-19, 21, 23, 25-26, 32, 34, 36, 40-41, 48, 50, 52, 73, 75, 83, 87, 99, 102, 108-109, 113, 117, 129, 132, 138, 143-144, 146-147, 149-150, 159-160, 163, 167, 175-176, 180, 191, 193, 197; Grandpa Bill, 5-8, 10, 12-15, 18-21, 23, 25, 27-28, 30-36, 40-45, 48, 50, 52, 54, 63-64, 72-73, 75-76, 81-83, 85, 87-88, 92-95, 97, 99-102, 104-105, 108-109, 111, 113-114, 117, 129, 132, 138-139, 143-144, 146-147, 153, 159-160, 163, 167-170, 175, 179-181, 187, 190-191, 193, 197
Reed, Doctor Rogers (Dock), 14, 24
Reed, Ed (Uncle Ed), 5
Reed, Enos, 8, 30
Reed, E. T., 20
Reed Family Reunions, 8
Reed, J. A., 20
Reed, Jimmy, 14, 17, 34, 41, 44, 99, 104
Reed, John (Uncle Sonny), 4-5, 90, 94, 197, 199
Reed, Kelvin, 186
Reed, Lem, 28, 32, 43, 52
Reed, Leon (Uncle Leon), 4, 6, 14
Reed, Mary Frances, 14
Reed, Melvin (Uncle Melvin), 4

Reed, Minnie, 2, 4, 24, 38, 54
Reed, Pleasant (Uncle Pleas), 12, 15, 23, 38, 41
Reed & Puryear Family Reunion, 7, 11, 25-26, 162, 169, 185, 187, 197
Reed, Rosalind, 7
Reed, Sam Houston, 20-21
Reed, Sarah Partee, 10, 14-15, 17, 19, 24, 26, 36-38, 73
Reed, Simpson, 2-5, 12, 14-15, 21, 24-25, 34, 38, 54, 197
Reed, Thomas Adison, 14
Reed, Wallace, 33-34
Reed, Willie, 14-15
Reed, Zalmon, 20
Reid, Alexander Mack, 71
Reid, Annie White, 76
Reid, Elizabeth, 71, 76
Reid, George, 67, 69-70
Reid, Hannah, 183
Reid, Hugh, 51, 70, 101
Reid, James, 71
Reid, James Caldwell, 71
Reid, Jane, 71
Reid, Joel, 183
Reid, John White, 83
Reid, Lemuel, 52, 64-66, 68, 71-73, 77, 82-85, 92, 97, 127, 129-130, 139, 152, 167-169, 172-174, 178-179, 181-183, 190
Reid, Lemuel IV, 173
Reid, Margaret, 70-71
Reid, Margery, 71, 135
Reid, Marilyn, 183
Reid, Melanie, 183
Reid, Oscar, 183
Reid Place, 72, 75-78, 80-81, 85, 177, 179-181, 201
Reid, Pleasant, 168
Reid, Rosie, 71
Reid, Samuel, 71, 167, 181
Reid, Samuel Orren (Bud), 74, 76, 85
Reid, Shelley, 172-173, 175, 183

Reid, Sophia Weston, 67-68, 72, 175, 183
Reid, Wayne, 65, 72-73, 76-77, 82, 85, 179
Reid, William, 174
Revolutionary War, 69
Richie's Funeral Home, 206
Rinda (slave), 51, 90, 94, 96-97, 101
Ripley, Mississippi, 42, 45-49, 53-56, 58-62, 117, 130, 139, 144, 147, 163, 184, 190, 214
Robertson County, Tennessee, 107
Rochester, New York, 151, 199
Rogers, Bill, 75
Rogers, Elizabeth, 60-61
*Roots*, 1-2, 5, 22
Ross, Georgia, 131
Rough House, 172-173
Rowan County, North Carolina, 51
Royal Land Grant, 69
Ruff, Sina Ella, 148, 150-151
Rust College, 53-54, 114, 147, 165-166
Rutherford, Susie, 145-146, 148

**S**

Saddler, John, 116
Sankofa, 35
Scotch-Irish, 67, 69-70
Scotland, 92
Selma, Alabama, 115
Senatobia, Mississippi, 8, 10, 18, 33, 93, 144, 149-150
Senegal, 9
Session book, 120, 125, 127-129, 131, 134, 167
Session House, 209
Shadrack (slave), 130
sharecropping, 4
Sheegog, Simon, 116
Shenandoah Valley, 67
Singletary, Rev. E. R., 74
slave churches, 133
slave galleries, 209

slave inventory, 90, 93, 105, 112, 206
slave schedule, 19, 20-21, 52, 95, 101-102, 104, 115, 117, 127, 141, 156
Smith's plantation, 106
Social Security, 110
*Somerset Homecoming*, 85
Somerville, Tennessee, 126
Songhai, 157
Sons of Allen Male Group, 201, 210
soundex, 13-14, 108-110
South Carolina African American Heritage Commission, 173
South Carolina Department of Archives and History (SCDAH), 87-88
South Carolina Department of Transportation, 170
Southaven, Mississippi, 186
Spartanburg, South Carolina, 126-129
Speer, Robert, 170
Spight, Frederick, 55, 57
Spight, Lewis, 55
St. Louis, Missouri, 8, 151, 192
St. Paul Methodist Church, 53-60, 130
St. Paul Board of Trustees, 57
Starkville, Mississippi, 22
Stono Rebellion, 198
Sunday School, 123
Susan Ebony (slave), 129
Swatawra Creek, 67
sycamore tree, 28, 33-34, 36, 175, 177

**T**

Talledega, Alabama, 122
Tate County, Mississippi, 2, 10, 12-14, 19, 21, 27, 33, 36, 40, 43, 52-53
Temple University, 9
Tennessee, 4, 8, 10-11, 15, 22, 33, 42, 49-50, 54, 56, 107, 110, 126, 150, 169, 185, 192

Texas, 107, 199
Thomas, Claude, 172, 174
Thomas, Susan Beckley, 146
Thompson, Bob, 135-136, 141
Tippah County, Mississippi, 22, 43, 47, 49, 53, 55-56, 62, 109
tobacco, 214
transatlantic slave trade, 70, 90, 158
Tulsa Race Riot, 171
Tupelo, Mississippi, 148, 150-151, 162, 164, 169
Turner, LaCorsha, 172
Turpin, Frank, 193, 212

# U

U.S. GenWeb, 145
Ulster, Ireland, 67
Union Army, 49, 109
Union County, Indiana, 70-71
Union soldier, 83
United States Colored Troops (USCT), 49, 83
University of Mississippi (Ole Miss), 116
Upper Long Cane Church, 51, 69-70, 119-122, 125-126, 130-131, 134, 164, 167, 175, 177, 183, 201, 208-209
Upper Long Cane cemetery, 175
Upper Mississippi Conference, 59

# V

Vargus, Ione D., 9
Vereen, Ben, 6
Voorhees, New Jersey, 151

# W

Walton-Raji, Angela, 22, 41, 55, 184
Ware, Lowry, 173
Warren County, Mississippi, 39
Washington, D.C., 46, 142, 182

The Washingtons of Wessyngton Plantation, 107
Waters, Kenneth L., 158
Watts, Thomas, 53
Weatherall, Eliza, 144
Wells, Alberta, 145
Westin Hotel, 194
White, Cowan, 53
White, Mingo, 131
White, Paul, 4
Williams, Rose-Marie, 170
Williamson, Sam, 117
Williamson, Sina, 117
Willis, Catherine, 172, 181
Wilson, Danny, 170
Wilson, Elizabeth Ann, 71
Wilson, Glasgow, 19, 32-33, 73, 92, 168
Wilson, Harvey, 76, 140
Wilson, Hawkins, 107
Wilson, J. H., 74
Wilson, John R. (J.R.), 71, 74, 76, 92, 167-168
Wilson, L. C., 76
Wilson, Leroy, 140
Wilson, Mary Reid, 71, 73
Wilson, Robert C., 71
Works Progress Administration, 131
Wright, Bernie, 173
Wright, Thomasina, 172

# Y

Young, Amanda, 42, 46, 49, 184
Young, Berry, 42, 46, 49
Young, Tandy, 48
Yoruba, 9, 199

# Z

Zion Church, Mississippi, 128-129

CPSIA information can be obtained at www.ICGtesting.com
Printed in the USA
LVOW07s1829290814

401515LV00002B/507/P

9 781463 725686